Understanding occam and the transputer

– through complete, working programs

David Ellison

SIGMA PRESS
Wilmslow, England

Typeset and Designed by Sigma Hi-Tech Services Ltd, Wilmslow, UK

Printed in Malta by
Interprint Ltd.

First published in 1991
Sigma Press, 1 South Oak Lane, Wilmslow, Cheshire SK9 6AR, UK

First printed 1991

ISBN: 1-85058-206-8

British Library Cataloguing in Publication Data
A CIP catalogue record for this book is available from the British Library

Preface

This book is aimed at advanced undergraduates and other people with substantial computing experience, who wish to develop and run their own occam programs on a network of transputers, as quickly as possible. Its philosophy is to present complete, working programs, rather than snatches of code illustrating salient points of occam. It starts with the simplest of programs on one transputer (to write a "hello" message to the screen), which gives experience of the folding editor and the compiler, and should take about fifteen minutes of effort. It then works through more advanced examples (chiefly based on the Newton-Raphson pipeline algorithm for extracting the square roots of 20000 integers), introducing occam concepts as necessary on the way, and ends with the Mandelbrot program "farmed out" on a network of several transputers. It is intended and strongly recommended that you learn about occam, the folding editor, configuration etc. by typing in and running each of these programs, so that at the end you should be in a strong position to carry on with the transputer on your own. The occam language is not described in its entirety, but sufficient is introduced as needed for the various programs. It is assumed that your transputer and network is hosted on an IBM PC or equivalent.

Chapter 1 introduces occam and the transputer, giving an understanding of how a pipeline program can be distributed on several transputers to increase throughput. A very simple "Hi there" program introduces a few occam concepts, such as `INT` variables, `SEQ` and input from channels.

Chapter 2 gives in full detail how to input this program into an `EXE` fold, using the folding editor, and then how to compile and run it on a single transputer.

Chapter 3 presents the Newton-Raphson program in two forms: as a sequential program (similar to one that might be written in Pascal), introducing replicators, `VAL`s, reals and scope; and also as a parallel one to introduce the `PAR` construct, `PROTOCOL`s and `CHAN`nels. The sequential program provides a benchmark timing, for comparison with other versions in Chapter 5. Since these programs are run on just one transputer (the host), of course no speed-up in operation is obtained.

Chapter 4 presents sufficient brief detail of the structure of the transputer to help understand the distribution of programs on a network. Again, a minimal program illustrates these points. It sends a signal to the network (consisting of one extra transputer!) which replies with a message that it is alive and kicking. Termination of programs is discussed and the `WHILE, IF,` and `ALT` constructors introduced. This program is first developed on the host transputer and then configured for the network. This involves explanation of `PLACE`ment, the association of channels with physical links, and the association of a program with a particular transputer. `PROGRAMs` and `SC` (separately compiled) procedures are needed for this. Details of the actual (physical) wiring connecting the transputer boards are given.

With the experience of this simple network, Chapter 5 describes the changes to the Newton-Raphson program so it can be placed on a network of `M` transputers, and the necessary configuration and rearrangement of the wiring. A minor modification allows initialising data to be broadcast through the network to all transputers; this means the same channel can communicate data of different types, for which variant protocols are needed. The last part of this chapter compares speed-up and efficiency of the network, with theoretical estimates derived from specifications found in the transputer manual.

Chapter 6 describes another common form of parallelism – a processor farm using the Mandelbrot set as an illustration. This involves routing data packets from transputer to transputer. In a farm each processor works on its own packet of data independent of all other such packets, the time of processing varying from packet to packet. The load balancing is automatic. The graphics of the IBM computer are used for displaying the Mandelbrot figures; this means the program has to be run as a "stand-alone" program, independent of the TDS server, using the `afserver` to communicate pixels to the screen via the BIOS of the IBM PC.

Again, some theoretical estimates for the processing/communication times are derived from the transputer specifications and compared with actual speed-ups. Often it is difficult to see the behaviour of the transputers in the network, but by colour coding each transputer, the graphics display can indicate the usage.

Chapter 7 covers debugging programs and networks; this includes, first, DIY, where print statements are inserted in the occam code; and, second, a description of the use of the debugger supplied with the TDS; and, finally, the `worm` which is a program that finds its way from transputer to transputer to check the integrity of the hardware.

The final Chapter gives a very brief coverage of some points not met in the main text of Chapters 1 to 7.

Appendix C gives the syntax of occam2. For people new to a language, dry syntax by itself can be hard to follow, so short, example snippets of occam are included. The syntax is also cross-referenced.

Appendix D is an *aide-memoire* for the folding editor, compiler, configurer etc.

The book is based on a set of lectures presented to a fourth year Science Degree course at Dundee Institute of Technology. Sections 5.6 to 5.7 and 6.7 and 6.9 are "the answers" to practical work set for the students. Equipment is a B004 board on an IBM XT, IBM AT or Zenith. The network is a B006 board, with just three T2 transputers. The program listings were produced using the Sheffield lister, and then kermitted to a VAX 11/780, where the page references were removed. Otherwise they are as developed.

I am very grateful for the help and facilities provided by Dundee Institute of Technology, in particular by the Department of Mathematical and Computer Sciences, the Microsystems Laboratory and the Reprographics Unit. Thanks are also due to many people at INMOS Ltd for providing the very useful technical notes, occam sources for several of their programs and general help with some of the problems I encountered.

Especial thanks also go to Patricia McKelvie, Angela Robertson, Audrey Cane and Jenny Leslie for word processing the manuscript and displaying unbounded patience in so doing.

David Ellison

Contents

1

Introduction to occam and the transputer

1.1 Overview

Occam and the transputer were designed hand-in-hand. Occam is a programming language for parallel processing, on a network of transputers. A transputer is a microcomputer, with its own local memory which can communicate with other transputers via four in-built links. It is a VLSI device with explicit hardware for supporting the occam mode of concurrency and the synchronisation of processes. A process is a software building block, and an occam program is an interconnected set of such processes.

The transputer is actually a family of similar microcomputers, with different attributes. For example, the T212 has a 16-bit architecture, the T414 32-bits, each with floating point arithmetic handled by software, while the T800 is 32-bits with a floating point unit incorporated into the microprocessor chip. Whilst having differing properties, all transputers in the family have the same instruction set, independent of wordlength. Of course, there are some variations in behaviour; for example, 32-bit real numbers on the T212 require two words and consequently real arithmetic will be slower.

Because the language and processor were designed hand-in-hand does not mean other languages cannot be run on transputers, nor that occam is restricted to the transputer. There are now several compilers available for conventional (sequential) languages such as Fortran, Pascal and C that will produce code to run on transputers. These, typically, have add-on features for dealing with parallelism. Further, alien languages can be embedded into occam code (Wayman, 1989). Occam at present is largely restricted to transputers, though there are sytems becoming available which provide compilation and debugging facilities for running occam code on a PC, entirely independent of transputers (for example, CODE 1989).

The aim of this book is to introduce you to parallelism via occam and a network of transputers. It enables you to run a series of programs (of increasing complexity) on various configurations of transputers, to demonstrate the increased performance (over a single transputer and over a single micro such as the IBM PC) that can follow from using a network of parallel processors.

Figures 1.1, 5.1 and 6.1 show typical problems (a pipeline for finding the square roots of integers and a processor farm for the Mandelbrot set) that can be run on a network of transputers and Tables 5.1 to 5.3 and 6.1 indicate the increase in performance. We shall see later (Section 4.4 and Chapter 5) the ways of delivering the various parts of the compiled occam program to the correct transputers. Essentially, the complete occam program is developed on a single (host) transputer and, when ready to run it on a network, you make minor modifications to the program indicating which parts are destined for which transputer. The transputer development system (TDS) then carries out this distribution for you.

An example is given below to illustrate this more clearly, but, first a few words about "front ending" a transputer. Chiefly for program development (but, often, for running programs, too) a transputer is connected to a computer (in our case an IBM PC). The IBM allows you to communicate with the transputer using the IBM's keyboard and screen (whilst the transputer is a microcomputer by itself, it is deaf and blind and so needs some such symbiotic arrangement). INMOS supply a variety of transputer boards to plug into an expansion slot of the IBM. The one used here is a B004 (pronounced "boo 4") containing one T414 transputer, memory and necessary bits and pieces to make things work. The combination of IBM and B004 is referred to as "The Host". The T414 is usually abbreviated to T4.

As an example showing how a problem can end up as an occam program running on several transputers, consider a pipeline for finding the square roots of numbers, using a Newton-Raphson scheme:

$$x^{(1)} := \text{starting value, well chosen (say } x/2)$$

FOR n = 1 TO 10

$$x^{(n+1)} = (x^{(n)} + x/x^{(n)})/2$$

At each iteration, an improved estimation $x^{(n+1)}$ to the square root of x is found, using the current estimation $x^{(n)}$ and x. Then, after 10 iterations, $x^{(11)}$ is taken as the accepted approximation to the square root. We can arrange this scheme as a pipeline, with 10 stages. For example, for x = 2, starting with $x^{(1)} = 1$, we have:

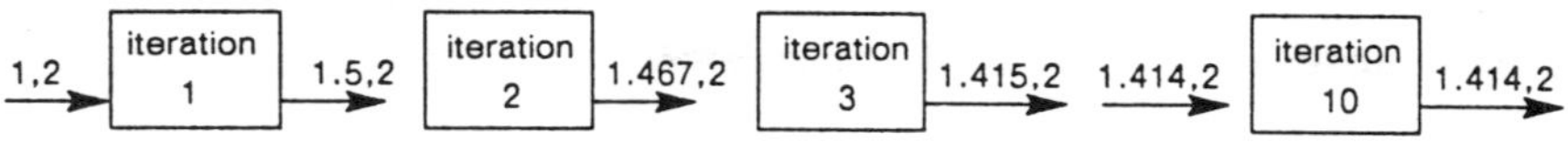

Figure 1.1 The Newton-Raphson Pipeline

Note that at each stage, both x and the latest estimate of the square root of x are passed on to the next stage. x and $x^{(n)}$ enter the nth stage, $x^{(n+1)}$ is calculated, then x and $x^{(n+1)}$ are passed on to the (n+1)th stage, as shown in Figure 1.2.

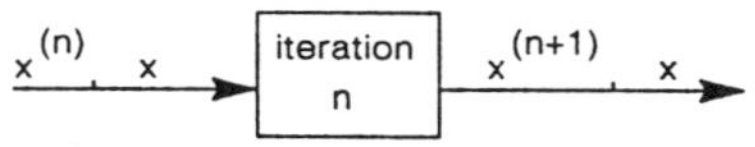

Figure 1.2 The nth iteration

The nth stage has now finished its task; the (n+1)th continues the processing in a similar fashion. The nature of the processing at each stage is identical and so the pseudocode for each stage can be written as follows:

```
input x and est
est := (est + x/est)/2
output x and est
```

Now, if we have 10 transputers available, we can devote one to each stage, each transputer having a compiled copy of and running this same program. Copies of the program can be sent down the pipeline from the host before processing starts.

Of course, with this arrangement, there is no speed-up in processing a single square root. However, if we wanted to compile a table of the square roots of the first 20000 integers, we feed in these one after the other; as soon as the first stage has passed its data to the second, the next integer and the initial approximation to its square root are fed into stage 1; and so on. Thus, at any one time, each stage of the pipeline is processing a different iteration for the square roots of several integers, in parallel. In this case, we could expect a speed-up of a factor of about 10 (the number of transputers in the pipeline).

1.2 Overview of occam

We do not elaborate occam in great detail - there are many useful books some of which are listed in the bibliography, and Appendix C gives a full, cross-referenced syntax with illustrative examples mostly taken from programs in this book. Assuming you have expertise in languages such as Pascal or MODULA-2, the major differences (such as `PAR` and `ALT` constructs) will be emphasised. Some minor ones should be clear, for example, `x := 0;` in Pascal may become `x := 0(REAL32)` in occam.

Before introducing the first occam program, a few notes on program structure in general are needed.

1.2.1 Programs and processes

This Section gives a very brief summary of some of the major features of occam; it is by no means complete. However, these and other features will be explained as they arise in programs.

An occam program is built up from processes which communicate with one another, and possibly with the outside world, through channels. Each process starts, performs a number of actions and then terminates. An action may be a set of sequential processes which are performed one after the other, or it may be a set of parallel processes which are executed "simultaneously". In fact, if they are run on the same processor, true simultaneity is not possible, but, instead, the parallel processes will be time sliced. Figure 1.3 shows a process, `P`, with two input channels, `C1` and `C2`, and one output channel, `C3`.

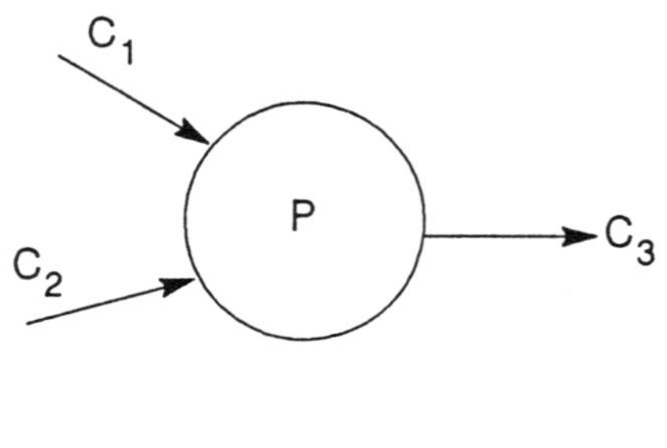

Figure 1.3 A process P, with two input and one output channels

occam has a small number of basic building blocks, known as primitive processes:

Primitive Processes		**Examples**
Input	(?)	`keyboard ? char`
Output	(!)	`screen ! number`
Assignment	(:=)	`est := x * Half`

Here, `keyboard` and `screen` are channels, and `char` and `number` variables.

Input

The input process `?` inputs a value from an occam channel and assigns it to the named variable, and then terminates. Thus, the first example will input a character along the channel `keyboard` into the variable named `char`.

Output

The output process `!` outputs the value of an expression along a named channel, so the second example sends a value `number` along the channel `screen`.

Assignment

Assignment operates much as in Pascal: the expression is evaluated and its value assigned to the named variable.

Note, unlike in Pascal, no ";" is needed at the end of "statements".

Types and declarations

`BOOL, BYTE, INT, INT16, INT32, INT64, REAL32, REAL64`

`BOOL` is Boolean. `INT` is an integer with word size dependent on the type of processor (e.g 16-bits on a T212, 32-bits on a T414). `INT16` is a 16-bit integer on any type of processor. Examples of declarations are:

```
INT16 number1, number2:
[10] BYTE message :
```

The first introduces two 16-bit integer variables called `number1` and `number2`, while the second declares an array `message` of size 10 of bytes.

In occam, the type precedes the list of names of variables of that type. Declarations can occur anywhere in an occam program, preceding the Section of code to which they apply. The `:` binds the variables to the following process. Arrays can have any number of dimensions, but their sizes must be fixed when they are declared. The dimension precedes the type.

Specifiers

`CHAN OF, VAL, PROC, PROTOCOL`

These allow channels, constants, procedures and protocols to be named.

CHAN OF

This allows a channel to be named, giving it a specified protocol. For example,

```
CHAN OF INT16 C1, C2, C3:
```

names the channels `C1, C2, C3` and allows them to transfer 16-bit integers.

```
CHAN OF BOOL keyboard:
```

allows the channel `keyboard` to transfer type `Boolean`.

VAL

VAL implements abbreviations, and has similarities to CONST in Pascal, though it is much more powerful. There are two types of abbreviation: ones which specify a name for an element, and ones which specify a name for an expression. For example,

```
VAL Two IS 2:
```

defines the constant Two to have the value 2; and

```
VAL y IS 2 * x:
```

specifies a name y for the expression 2 * x.

PROC

PROC introduces a procedure, a named process, much as PROCEDURE does in Pascal. In general, the format is

```
PROC name(parameter list)
  procedure body
:
```

where the : indicates the end of the procedure, in the same column as the P of PROC. For example,

```
PROC Mult.by.const(REAL32 x, VAL REAL32 const)
  x := const * x
:
```

defines a procedure Mult.by.const. Note, unlike Pascal, the "variable" parameter in occam (x here) does not require the use of the word VAR. However, "value" parameters (const here) must be preceded by VAL.

An "instance" is a call of a procedure; for example,

```
Mult.by.const(z, Epsilon)
```

PROTOCOL

A protocol can be given a name:

```
PROTOCOL chars IS [10] BYTE:
```

so that, for example, channels C1, C2, C2 could be declared:

```
CHAN OF chars C1, C2, C3:
```

Constructors

`SEQ, PAR, ALT, IF, WHILE`

These are used to combine primitive processes into larger ones, which may themselves be combined into larger processes still.

SEQ

The `SEQ` constructor causes its component processes to be executed one after the other, and must be used if you want several processes to be executed in sequence. For example, referring to Figure 1.3, the process

```
CHAN OF INT16 C1, C2, C3:
INT16 number1, number2:
SEQ
  C1 ? number1
  C2 ? number2
  C3 ! number1 + number2
```

will first input `number1` from the channel `C1`, then input `number2` from `C2` and then finally output their sum along channel `C3`. The program will wait until a number appears on channel `C1` before moving on to execute the input on channel `C2`; and so on. Of course, there will exist other processes which at some time should send data along `C1` and `C2` to this receiving process. Note that the extent of the `SEQ` process is delineated by the indentation of precisely two columns, and that no `BEGIN`s or `END`s are needed or provided in occam.

PAR

With the `PAR` constructor the component processes are executed in parallel. In fact, as noted above, on a single transputer, this will be simulated parallelism. So, for example, we could write

```
CHAN OF INT16 C1, C2, C3:
INT16 number1, number2:
PAR
  C1 ? number1
  C2 ? number2
```

but not

```
INT16 number:
PAR
  number := 12
  number := 96
```

This is illegal occam: `number` cannot be given the values 12 and 96 simultaneously.

ALT

The ALT constructor chooses between input channels, taking the one that is ready first, and executes the corresponding process. Then the ALT is terminated. For example, we can write a simple multiplexor:

```
[10] BYTE message:
CHAN OF [10] BYTE C1, C2, C3:

ALT
  C1 ? message
    C3 ! message

  C2 ? message
    C3 ! message
```

in which a message is conveyed along channel C3 from whichever of channels C1 and C2 first has a message to send. Thus, if C2 is ready first, its complete message of 10 bytes will be sent along C3 before the ALT is terminated. On another occasion, C1 might be ready first. The inputs here are referred to as guards.

IF

Similar to the IF statement in Pascal, the IF constructor is a conditional but differs in that it performs just one of a number of possible actions, depending on a sequence of tests, and then the construct terminates. For example,

```
IF
  condition1
    P1
  condition2
    P2
  ...
```

means that the process P1 is done if condition1 is true, otherwise P2 is done if condition2 is true, and so on.

```
IF
  x > 5
    y := 2 * y
  x <= 5
    SKIP
```

doubles y only if x is greater than 5.

WHILE

As in Pascal,

```
WHILE condition
  P
```

repeats the process `P` until the condition becomes false.

As shown in Figure 1.4, processes can be connected together into larger processes:

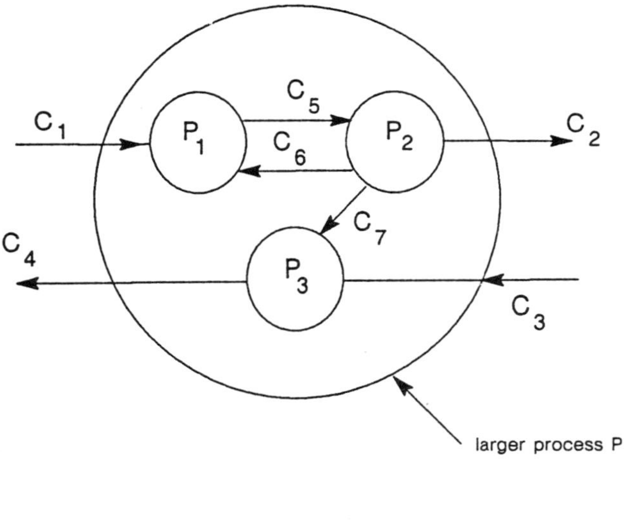

Figure 1.4 Processes connected to form a larger process

These processes may be run on a single transputer or on a network of transputers (c.f. the Newton-Raphson program above). For example, `P1`, `P2` and `P3` could all be on one transputer; or `P1` and `P2` could be on one transputer with `P3` on a second, the channel `C7` between the two processors being via transputer links. To determine the distribution of processes to processors is not an easy task and several examples will be met in later chapters.

1.2.2 Channels

A channel allows one-way, synchronised communication between two concurrent processes i.e. a "rendezvous". "One-way" means that one process must output data along the channel and the other must input it, but transfer of information cannot take place in the reverse direction. The processes are synchronised in that both processes must be ready before the data can be transferred. If one is ready before the other, the process that is ready first will wait until the second one is ready. Synchronisation is handled automatically by occam on the transputer. The rendezvous has the advantage that buffering of data is not needed for communication.

Channels can be "hard" or "soft". A hard channel is implemented on the input/ output links of the transputer, soft channels are implemented by software only.

1.3 A first program - printing "Hi There"

Listing 1.1 shows a very simple occam program which we explain below; all it does is write the message "Hi there" to the screen.

```
-- Writes "Hi There" on the screen
#USE userio

INT Any:
SEQ
  write.full.string (screen, "Hi There")
  keyboard ? Any
```

Listing 1.1 A simple occam program

1.3.1 Stages in writing and running a program on the host

The next chapter describes in detail how to input and run this program. The steps for any program running on the host are:

(i) use the TDS (Transputer Development System) editor to input the program into a file

(ii) Check it for syntax errors

(iii) Compile it (linking follows automatically)

(iv) Load it

(v) Run it

1.4 Explanation of the program

Comments

These can be introduced anywhere in a program by `--` but they must have the indentation of the following line.

Library

The `#USE userio` indicates the program uses some procedures found in the library `USERIO.TSR` located in an MS-DOS directory. The system automatically knows the location of this library. In this program, the only procedure is the `write.full.string`. The `.TSR` extension indicates an occam source code file.

Variables

```
INT Any:
```

This declares a variable `Any` of type integer (32-bits on a T4, 16 on a T2; a small point but note it well for later, in Chapters 5 and 6).

Note that in occam the type precedes the list of names of variables of that type. The colon is part of the declaration binding it to the following process.

SEQ

This indicates the following processes are to be executed in sequence (contrast `PAR` in Chapter 3). Note also that the lines following `SEQ` are indented precisely two characters; occam insists on indentation after every constructor word.

Note: there is no `BEGIN` or `END` for grouping "statements" as in Pascal, the indentation following a constructor being sufficient. One might think this would lead to programming problems, but when used sensibly in conjunction with folds (see next Chapter), the clarity of programs is not effected. In any case, the folding editor keeps a careful check on the correctness of indentation.

Writing to screen

There are many procedures for writing strings, integers, reals etc. in `USERIO.TSR`. `screen` is a reserved channel name, which in this case clearly indicates the output is to go to the screen. Any other relevant channel name could be used, if required.

Input

```
keyboard ? Any
```

This waits for some input on the `keyboard` channel, which is read into the variable `Any`. When running, this program will not terminate until a key on the keyboard is pressed. Without this process, the output would flash on the screen and disappear before you have time to read it, since when a program finishes running, the output is cleared and you are returned to the TDS.

2

Inputting and running the first program

This Chapter describes how to use the folding editor to type in a program, and then how to compile and run it, on the single (host) transputer. The program is the one listed in Section 1.3, but it first requires some further manipulation into a form suitable for running on the host. The complete folds necessary are given in Listings 2.1 to 2.4; how to produce them is described later.

```
...F TOPLEVEL.TOP
...F HITHERE.TOP
```

Listing 2.1 .TOP level folds

```
{{{F HITHERE.TOP
... EXE HiThere.tsr
}}}
```

Listing 2.2 The HITHERE.TOP fold opened

```
{{{F EXE HiThere.tsr
...F HiThere.tsr
...F code
...F descriptor
...F link
...F debug
...F CODE EXE HiThere.tsr
}}}
```

Listing 2.3 The EXE HiThere.tsr fold set

```
{{{F HiThere.tsr
-- Writes "Hi There" on the screen
#USE userio

INT Any:
SEQ
  write.full.string (screen, "Hi There")
  keyboard ? Any
}}}
```

Listing 2.4 The F HiThere.tsr fold

In this Section frequent references to the various keys of the keyboard are made. Our convention for the IBM is:

@Fn	– press the ALT key, and function key n, simultaneously
@n	– press the ALT key and the digit n (above QWERTY row), simultaneously
kpn	– press the key digit n on the keypad at the right hand side of keyboard
SFn	– press <SHIFT> and function key n, simultaneously
^Fn	– press <CONTROL> and function key n, simultaneously
<TAB>	– the tab key
<DELETE>	– delete left key, above the <RETURN>

2.1 Starting the TDS

All occam programs must be contained in `.TOP` files. For example:

```
tds2 -t HiThere.top
```

will create a new file `HITHERE.TOP` and leave you in the TDS, displaying a list of all `.TOP` files (See Listing 2.1). If you do not want a new file, `tds2` will start up the system, and you can then enter the one of your choice.

2.2 Introduction to the folding editor

The *aide-memoire* in Appendix D contains summarised details and a keyboard layout; enough details are given in this Section to allow you to type in the "Hi There" program.

WARNING: always ensure the < NUMERIC LOCK> is off, otherwise the keypad keys will not function!

Once in the TDS, the editor is already waiting for use. It contains the usual editor functions such as cursor control and deletion (see the *aide-memoire* in Appendix D for details).

2.2.1 Folds

The TDS editor differs from others in that it is a "folding" editor, a very useful feature which encourages top-down program design. Folding hides away the body of the text of a fold, leaving only the "headings" displayed. Folds are indicated by ... foldname; see Listings 2.1 to 2.4, for examples, in which some folds are progressively opened for display.

2.2.2 Entering and leaving folds

If you want to see the details hidden away you can "enter" a chosen fold by placing the cursor on the fold line and pressing the keypad 7 key (kp7). For example, Listing 2.2 shows the display on entering the `HITHERE.TOP` fold; the fold line `...F HITHERE.TOP` is replaced by `{{{F HITHERE.TOP`, followed by the contents; and the end of the opened fold is indicated by `}}}`.

To leave a fold, press kp9, at any line in the fold – the brackets are removed and the three full stops/periods (`...`) reappear.

2.2.3 Creating and removing folds

You can enclose existing text in a fold, or create new (empty) folds.

Move the cursor to the appropriate line and press 0 on the keypad (kp0). `{{{` will appear, indicating the top crease of the fold. Move the cursor to where you want the bottom crease to be (if it is to be an empty fold you don't need to move the cursor); pressing 0 will produce `...`, indicating a fold line. Now type in a useful name of your choice.

To remove a fold (but not delete the contents), place the cursor on the fold line and press ^kp9 (i.e. <CONTROL> and kp9 simultaneously).

2.3 Exercise – Typing in the "Hi There" Program

Full details of all key presses to type in the "Hi There" program are given here. (5 minutes typing time). They are given as a guide – such detail will be omitted later.

Action	**Key Presses**
Enter TDS with new `.TOP` file	tds2 -t HiThere.top
Move cursor to `...F HITHERE.TOP` fold	kp↓
Enter fold. `"No current UTIL"` is just a reminder that you have not yet loaded the Compile/Configure Utilities	kp7
So you can type in text, move }}} down	<RETURN> kp↑
Create a new (and empty) fold `... HiThere.tsr` (do not type `EXE` as in Listing 2.2 – that will be added later – see Section 2.6)	kp0 kp0 HiThere.tsr
Enter fold and move to new line	kp7 <RETURN> kp↑
Type in program as given in Listing 2.4, remembering: (i) occam is case sensitive; (ii) correct indentation	

2.3.1 Indenting

To indent two columns press space bar twice (note that the tab key does not tab). After typing in a line and pressing <RETURN>, the cursor returns to the indented position of the previous line. To outdent (the opposite of indent!), use the delete left key (the "normal" <DELETE> key – marked <--).

To change indentation:

(i) too much indentation – place cursor at the first character of the line of text and delete spaces (F7 <DELETE>)

(ii) too little indentation – F7 <spaces>

(iii) several lines need changing – place lines in a temporary fold, adjust its indentation and remove the fold.

2.4 Compiling, linking and running

To compile a program, you must first file it as a `.TSR` file and then turn this into an `...EXE` fold, to which the compiler is applied. Filing a fold makes a separate disk file of your chosen fold; the `EXE` is a "fold set" (see Listing 2.3 and Section 2.6.1) which will eventually contain compiled code etc. necessary for running your program.

You must first load the compiler utilities (a package including the checker, compiler and other features) by pressing SF5.

2.5 Filing a fold

❑ Exit from your program till you reach `... Hi There.tsr` (press kp9 repeatedly)

❑ File fold – place the cursor on the fold line (it should in this case already be there) and press SF2.

An "F" indicating a filed fold should appear: `...F HiThere.tsr`.

2.6 Creating an *EXE* fold set

To turn your program so far into a "compilation unit" ready for checking, compiling or running on the single (host) transputer, you have to make it an `...EXE` fold as shown in Listing 2.2.

There are several types of compilation units, for example, `SC` (Separately Compiled), `EXE` (Executable), `PROGRAM` (for a program for distribution on the network), `LIB` (for libraries), all of which can be compiled independently of other compilation units.

❑ place cursor (if not already there) on `...F HiThere.tsr` fold

❑ make it an `EXE` fold by pressing @7 (that is, the 7 of the digits above the QWERTY row – all utilities use those keys. **Beware:** avoid @F7 – delete a line, though you do get a second chance).

A fold is displayed with the default compilation unit probably set to `SC` (after the `IS`); change this to `EXE,` by pressing `<TAB>` as often as necessary.

The default will now remain an `EXE` until you change it.

2.6.1 Fold sets

The `EXE` fold is now a "fold set" – a fold containing one or more subsidiary folds used or produced by the utility (the compiler, in this case) (See Listing 2.3). The "code" (a file stored on disk as `HITHERE.DCD`) is the compiled occam code; "descriptor" (`.DDS` extension) identifies the compiler used (e.g. whether for a target T4 or T2) and contains information about the compilation; "link" (`.DLK` extension) contains linking information; "debug" (`.DDB`) has data needed for debugging a program, if needed later; and, finally, `"CODE EXE"` is the compiled, linked executable file (`.CEX`). These folds cannot be read by entering them.

2.7 Checking the syntax

You can check for any errors in syntax at any stage of development of a program, before compiling it. Apply the checker to the filed fold `...F HiThere.tsr` by pressing `@1`.

On its first use, the TDS presents a menu with several options for you to change, if you wish; at present accept the proferred defaults, by exiting the compiler fold.

2.7.1 Syntax errors

When the checker finds an error it displays the appropriate program text, leaving the cursor on the offending line with an error message at the top of the screen. Correct the error, exit the fold (it takes you back to the `...F HiThere.tsr`) and reapply the checker, until all errors are eliminated.

2.8 Compiling and linking

Now you are ready to compile – use `@2`. Linking will follow automatically on a successful compilation.

2.9 Loading and running

❑ place cursor on the `...EXE` fold

❑ get code – F5

❑ run code – F6

Don't forget that you must press any key to terminate the program successfully.

3

Pipeline program for the Newton-Raphson method

This Chapter introduces further occam ideas, chief of which are replication, `VAL` and `PAR`; it also compares a parallel version of the Newton-Raphson method with a sequential one, running on the host transputer.

The sequential version introduces replicated `SEQ`, `VALs`, and `REALs` and provides a timing benchmark. The parallel program in fact runs more slowly because of the overhead associated with implementing parallel processes on one transputer. Chapter 5 redresses this imbalance.

3.1 Sequential Newton-Raphson Method on the host transputer

Listings 3.1 to 3.3 show the Newton-Raphson program folds for printing in sequence the square roots of the first R (= 5) integers, using N (= 10) iterations; output on the screen is as in Figure 3.1 A pseudocode equivalent is:

```
R = 5, N = 10
FOR r = 1 TO R

   x:=r, est:=0.5x                  -- feed in integers

   FOR n = 1 TO N                   -- main iterations
      est:= (est + x/est)/2

   Write x and est                  -- print square roots
```

3.2 Explanation of the program

Listing 3.1 shows the outer folds, which should now be familiar, for the sequential Newton-Raphson program (named PIPESEQ).

```
...F PIPESEQ.TOP

{{{F PIPESEQ.TOP
... EXE pipeseq.tsr
}}}

{{{ EXE pipeseq.tsr
...F pipeseq.tsr
...F code
...F descriptor
...F link
...F debug
...F CODE EXE pipeseq.tsr
}}}

{{{F pipeseq.tsr

#USE userio
... Comments on program
... VALs etc
SEQ
  ... running
  ... main program
  ... finished and pause
}}}
```

Listing 3.1 The outer folds for the sequential Newton-Raphson program (PIPESEQ)

3.2.1 Constants (`VAL`)

The specification:

```
VAL name IS value:
```

assigns a constant value to the name, much as `CONST` does in Pascal. Thus, in Listing 3.2, on the next page, `VAL Half IS 0.5 (REAL32) :` gives the value 0.5 to the name `Half`. The `(REAL32)`, in which the brackets are essential, ensures that 0.5 is a 32-bit floating-point real (you can also use `REAL64`). `Half` is thus a 32-bit real constant.

`VAL R IS 5:` declares the constant `R` to be integer 5, the number of bits being automatically determined by the type of transputer for which the program is compiled (T2 is 16-bits, T4 32).

```
{{{ Comments on program
-- A Newton-Raphson program for extracting the square roots of
-- the first R integers. No parallelism involved.

-- N is the number of iterations to be used.
}}}

{{{ VALs etc
VAL Half IS 0.5 (REAL32):
VAL R IS 5:
VAL N IS 10:
}}}

{{{ running
write.full.string (screen, "Started running --")
newline (screen)
}}}

{{{ main program
SEQ r = 1 FOR R
  REAL32 x, est:
  SEQ
    ... feed in integers
    ... main iterations
    ... print square roots
}}}

{{{ finished and pause
INT Any:
SEQ
  write.full.string (screen, "Finished running -- ")
  keyboard ? Any

}}}
```

Listing 3.2 The folds of Listing 3.1 expanded (PIPESEQ)

3.2.2 Replication of processes

You will recall that the program finds the square roots of the first R integers. In Listing 3.2, in the main program fold, the line:

```
SEQ r = 1 FOR R
```

means we make R replicas of the following process and execute them in sequence. The general form is:

```
SEQ index = base FOR count
  process
```

The index variable (`r`, in the example) takes on values, starting with the base, in steps of 1, i.e. 1, 2, . . . , R, in this case. The type of the index is by default `INT` (integer) and this need not and should not be specified elsewhere. Note that the `FOR` is not quite the same as in Pascal; "base" and "count" must not be confused with "start" and "finish". For example:

```
SEQ r = 0 FOR 3
```

implies `r` takes the three values 0, 1, 2, in turn, and not 0, 1, 2, 3 as you would expect from the Pascal:

```
FOR r := 0 TO 3 DO
```

The `SEQ n = 1 FOR N` (in the `main iterations` fold of Listing 3.3) replicates its process `est := ((est + x/est)) * Half)` N times, i.e. carries out N Newton-Raphson iterations for each of the R integers.

3.2.3 Variable declaration and scope

In Listing 3.2, in the `main program` fold:

```
REAL32 x,est:
```

defines the variables `x, est` to be of type `REAL32`. These are local to the process (which may include subprocesses) immediately following their specification; indentation delineates the scope.

3.2.4 Type conversion

In the fold, `feed in integers` of Listing 3.3:

```
x := (REAL32 ROUND r)
```

x is of type `REAL32`, and `r` is, by default, `INT`; thus we use `ROUND` to convert `r` to `REAL32`.

```
{{{ feed in integers
x := (REAL32 ROUND r)
est := x * Half
}}}

{{{ main iterations
SEQ n = 1 FOR N
  est := ((est + (x/est)) * Half)
}}}

{{{ print square roots
... VALs
SEQ
  write.full.string (screen, "x = ")
  write.real32 (screen, x, Ip, Dp)
  write.full.string (screen, "sqrt(x) = ")
  write.real32 (screen, est, Ip, Dp)
  newline (screen)

}}}

{{{ VALs
VAL Ip IS 5:
VAL Dp IS 3:
}}}
```

Listing 3.3 The feed in integers, main iterations and print folds (PIPESEQ)

3.2.5 Operators and parentheses

All operators have the same priority in occam so we must use parentheses around every component operation in a complex expression, thereby establishing the order of evaluation. Thus `est := (est + x/est) * Half` is incorrect and fails at compilation. `(x/est)` is a component operation and so is `(est + (x/est))`. It is very easy to forget this – beware!

3.2.6 write.real32

In Listing 3.3, in the fold `print square roots`, `write.real32` is a procedure in `userio.tsr` and `Ip` and `Dp` refer to the number of digits before and after the decimal point of the real number.

3.3 Running the program

This takes 15 minutes typing time. First, create a new `.TOP` file – you will have to leave the TDS system to do this if you are already in it. Use "tds2 – t pipeseq.top". Then type the program in and get it working; the folds are shown in Listings 3.1 to 3.3. You can save some typing by copying the first `write.full.string` line and making the minor changes to produce the other lines:

3.3.1 Copying and moving lines of text

Move the cursor to the line to be copied, and press F4; a copy appears. Move it to the required position by first placing it in the move buffer (F3) and then repositioning the cursor; press F3 again to empty the buffer. For more copies, repeat this procedure.

3.3.2 Benchmark timings

Run the program for the first 20000 integers, for example. Some sample output is shown in Figure 3.1. You can use a stopwatch to time it, at present, though later the internal clock can be used. (You can include the extra code for this now – see Chapter 6 – but be it on your own head – it is worthwhile keeping things simple). You will first have to change `R` to 20000 in the program, but do not yet recompile and run it, since, if you do, you will have to sit watching 20000 lines of output.

3.3.3 COMMENTs

You could remove the write statements from the program, but it is better is to comment them out, in case you want them later. The TDS provides a very useful facility for this. Move the cursor to the `... print square roots` fold and press @0. The resulting `... COMMENT` fold is ignored by the compiler, but you can still edit its contents if you wish. To remove the `... COMMENT` use ^kp9.

3.3.4 Interrupting running programs

If you have to stop a program press <CONTROL><BREAK> simultaneously. You can then either quit (<ESC>) or re-boot the TDS (space bar). You will then have to reload any utility you need.

```
Started running --
x =        1.0  sqrt(x)  =     1.0
x =        2.0  sqrt(x)  =     1.414
x =        3.0  sqrt(x)  =     1.732
x =        4.0  sqrt(x)  =     2.0
x =        5.0  sqrt(x)  =     2.236
Finished running --
```

Figure 3.1 The Output from the Newton-Raphson Program

3.4 A parallel Newton-Raphson program on the host transputer

We introduce `PAR`, replicated `PAR`, `PROTOCOL` and `CHAN` in this Section.

The Newton-Raphson sequential program can be rewritten using several parallel processes, which can be run on the host. But what is the point? There can be no speed-up, and, indeed, there is a slow down because of the overhead involved in implementing the parallelism on one transputer (see Table 5.2, in Chapter 5). It is, in fact, easier to develop a program destined for a network of transputers on the host, since it avoids much time-consuming effort with the network at the debugging stage. Conceptionally, having written a program for a single machine, it is an "easy task" to convert the program into one suitable for running on the network: for example, compare Listings 3.6 and 3.7 with Listings 5.4 and 5.5, where the essential changes are the `PAR`s have been replaced by `PLACED PAR`. However, this "easy task" is not always as straight forward as often is claimed; the more "sensible" version of the Newton-Raphson program is given in Listings 5.1 to 5.6, where we had to change the occam code to make more efficient use of the transputer network (see in particular Listing 5.6). We also had to arrange to have the `feed` and `bleed` processes on the host transputer. Unless, at the development stage, one keeps quite clear what the eventual configuration will be, and writes the program accordingly, then there may have to be a fairly substantial rewrite of the program to transfer it to the network, so that it will run efficiently.

3.5 Processes for the parallel Newton-Raphson program

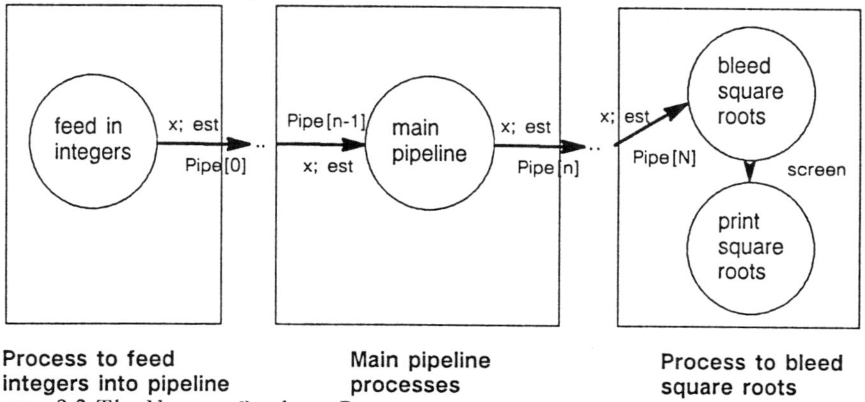

Figure 3.2 The Newton-Raphson Processes

The main pipeline processes (Figure 3.2) running in parallel are identical – they all perform the same calculation, but on different data, the nth one carrying out the nth iteration. Input `(x; est)` from the previous process is along the channel

`Pipe[n - 1]`, the iteration is then done and the output (`x` and the new `est`) sent along `Pipe[n]`. The `feed in integers` process generates the integers, as before, but passes `x` and `est` to the first pipeline process along channel `Pipe[0]`. The last process bleeds the numbers from the pipeline (`Pipe[N]`) and prints the results on the screen.

3.6 Explanation of the PIPEPAR program

Listings 3.4 to 3.7 show the occam folds for the parallel pipeline; Listing 3.4 with the exception of `PROTOCOL`, should be familiar by now.

```
...F PIPESEQ.TOP
...F PIPEPAR.TOP

{{{F PIPEPAR.TOP
... EXE pipepar.tsr

}}}

{{{ EXE pipepar.tsr
...F pipepar.tsr
...F code
...F descriptor
...F link
...F debug
...F CODE EXE pipepar.tsr
}}}

{{{F pipepar.tsr

#USE userio
... Comments on program
... VALs etc
... CHANs and PROTOCOL

SEQ
  ... running
  ... main program
  ... finished and pause

}}}
```

Listing 3.4 The outer folds for the parallel Newton-Raphson program (PIPEPAR)

The comments have changed appropriately, while the folds `VALs`, `running` and `finished and pause` remain the same.

3.6.1 PROTOCOL

See Listing 3.5, in the fold `CHANs and PROTOCOL`. The two reals, `x` and `est`, are to be passed along the channels connecting the parallel processes. To enable this, we define a `PROTOCOL` describing the structure of the data package, where x.est is the name given to the `PROTOCOL;` the data package consists of two 32-bit reals.

```
{{{ Comments on program
-- A Newton-Raphson program for extracting the square roots
-- of the first R integers. Parallel program for host
-- transputer.

-- N is the number of iterations to be used.
}}}

{{{ VALs etc
VAL Half IS 0.5 (REAL32):
VAL R IS 5:
VAL N IS 10:
}}}

{{{ CHANs and PROTOCOL
PROTOCOL x.est IS REAL32; REAL32:
[N+1] CHAN OF x.est Pipe:
}}}

{{{ running
write.full.string (screen, "Started running --")
newline (screen)
}}}

{{{ main program
PAR
  ... feed in integers to pipeline
  ... main pipeline
  ... bleed square roots
}}}

{{{ finished and pause
INT Any:
SEQ
  write.full.string (screen, "Finished running -- ")
  keyboard ? Any
}}}
```

Listing 3.5 The folds of Listing 3.4 expanded (PIPEPAR)

3.6.2 CHANnels

Since N is 10,

```
[N + 1] CHAN OF x.est Pipe:
```

defines 11 channels named `Pipe[0]` to `Pipe[10]`, which carry data according to `PROTOCOL x.est`.

3.6.3 PAR

In the `main program` fold, `PAR` indicates that the following processes are to be run in parallel. These are the feeding in of integers into the pipeline, the Newton-Raphson iterations and the bleeding of the pipeline (albeit, as above, on different data).

3.6.4 Synchronisation of the pipeline

The replicated `SEQ r = 1 FOR R` now appear in each of these three folds within the `PAR` (see Listings 3.6 and 3.7); they control the synchronised processing of the square rooted numbers. There is a kind of coordinated heart beat in each of the processes at which all the `x.est` data pulse on "simultaneously" to their next process – hence the term "systolic" in reference to the human heart beat. Remember, there is no communication between any two processes until both are ready. Because the replicated `SEQ`s are in `PAR` no data can be passed on until all of them are ready to communicate, for each value of `r`. Of course, on a single transputer "simultaneous" is simulated; on a network there is true simultaneity.

```
{{{ feed in integers to pipeline
SEQ r = 1 FOR R
  REAL32 x, est:
  SEQ
    x := (REAL32 ROUND r)
    est := x * Half
    Pipe[0] ! x; est
}}}

{{{ main pipeline
PAR n = 1 FOR N
  Input IS Pipe[n-1]:
  Output IS Pipe[n]:

  ... nth iteration
}}}
```

Listing continued on next page

```
{{{ bleed square roots
SEQ r = 1 FOR R
  REAL32 x, est:
  SEQ
    Pipe[N] ? x; est
    ... print square roots

}}}
```

Listing 3.6 The feed integers, main pipeline and bleed folds (PIPEPAR)

One might think that the replicated `SEQ`s could be removed from the inside of the processes and placed before the `PAR`, around all of them, in the following way:

```
SEQ r = 1 FOR R
  PAR
    ...feed
    ...main
    ...bleed
```

What would be the effect of this? The first integer, 1, would enter the pipeline and be processed by all stages of the `PAR`, before the `SEQ` could feed "2" into the pipeline. This is true, since the `feed` process starts first, while, through lack of data, neither `main` nor `bleed` can. Then, `feed` passes its data to `main` which can now immediately start (remember they are in parallel); all stages of the `PAR` must be completed before `r` becomes 2. In other words while the program would function, each integer has to pass through the entire pipeline before the next even begins its journey.

3.6.5 Pipe[0] ! x;est

In the `feed in integers` fold shown in Listing 3.6:

```
Pipe[0]! x;est
```

sends the data, as regulated by the protocol for this channel (`Pipe[0]`), to the receiving process, the first of the pipeline, when it is ready.

3.6.6 Replicated PAR

In Listing 3.6, in the `main pipeline` fold:

```
PAR n = 1 FOR N
```

means we make N replicas of the following process, each of which runs in parallel with all the others.

3.6.7 Abbreviations

In the `main pipeline` fold:

```
Input IS Pipe[n-1]:
```

defines an abbreviation for the element `Pipe[n-1]`, whose value depends on that of `n`. Thus, `Input` will refer to `Pipe[0]`, `Pipe[1]`, `Pipe[2]`, ..., as `n` goes from 1 to N. Note that `VAL Input IS Pipe[n-1]:` is illegal – `VAL` cannot be used when abbreviating elements.

```
{{{ nth iteration

SEQ r = 1 FOR R
  REAL32 x, est:

  SEQ
    Input ? x; est
    est := ((est + (x/est)) * Half)
    Output ! x;est
}}}

{{{ print square roots
... VALs
SEQ
  write.full.string (screen, "x = ")
  write.real32 (screen, x, Ip, Dp)
  write.full.string (screen, "sqrt(x) = ")
  write.real32 (screen, est, Ip, Dp)
  newline (screen)
}}}

{{{ VALs
VAL Ip IS 5:
VAL Dp IS 3:
}}}
```

Listing 3.7 The nth iteration and print folds (PIPEPAR)

3.7 Running the program

This takes about 25 minutes of typing. Create a new `.TOP` file called `PIPEPAR.TOP`. To avoid considerable retyping, you can copy the sequential program of Section 3.3 and modify it, for which you will need the file utilities, as follows:

3.7.1 File utilities and copying files

Autoload the file utilities by:

❑ enter `PIPEPAR.TOP`

❑ autoload utilities – SF5

❑ select file utilities – @F5

You can then copy `PIPESEQ.TSR` into a file of the same name in `PIPEPAR.TOP` and change the file name to `PIPEPAR.TSR`:

❑ create an empty file in `PIPEPAR.TOP` – kp0, kp0

❑ give it the name of the file you are copying – `PIPESEQ.TSR`

❑ copy – @2

❑ change its name:

(a) replace `SEQ` of `PIPESEQ.TSR` by `PAR`

(b) @4

This will avoid accidental deletion of the original `PIPESEQ.TSR`.

3.7.2 Copying several lines

You will need to copy the lines:

```
SEQ r = 1 FOR R
  REAL32 x,est:
```

to several places. The method is to place these two lines in a buffer and copy to where you need it, as many times as you wish. In fact, two buffers are used, one with the F3 and another with the @F3, as follows:

❑ remove the lines to be copied into a buffer: place cursor on first line and press @F3, as many times as needed

❑ copy the lines in place, immediately:

(a) put buffer – SF3

(b) copy fold into buffer for further copying – F4, F3.

(c) remove fold – ^kp9

❏ copy elsewhere:

(a) move cursor to required position

(b) F3, F4

(c) repeat (a) and (b) as often as required

3.7.3 Search and replace

These functions are not resident in the editor, but are included with the compiler. @8 searches for a string but does not replace; @9 replaces the string you have just found using @8. The first time you use @8, you get a menu asking you for a search string; move the cursor to between the double double quotes "" and type in the string you want. If you intend to replace (as opposed to just searching) type in a replace string on the next line, too. Then exit the fold and you will be at the first occurrence of the search string after the point you started at. Press @9 if you wish to replace; @8 if you don't but want to search for further occurrences.

If, later, you want to change the search/replace strings, enter the Toolkit fold (@F1), enter the Search and Replace fold and make the changes.

3.8 Timings

Once the program is working, change R to 20000 and again time the program. Do not forget to `COMMENT` out the `...Print` fold, first.

Exercises

1. Obtain benchmark timings for the Newton-Raphson program written in Pascal on the IBM PC, with and without a co-processor. Use values of N (the number of iterations used in calculating the square roots) = 5, 10, 20, 40 and 80, for R = 20000 integers. Use a stopwatch. Estimate the number of Flops by counting the number of floating point operations involved (see Table 5.1).

2. Obtain the equivalent timings to Exercise 1 using the host transputer alone by running the sequential program `PIPESEQ.TOP` (see Table 5.2). For each value of N, you will have to recompile the program, before running it. Also, for each N, display the memory usage by using @F2 (see Section 5.7.2 and Table 5.6).

3. Repeat Exercise 2 for the parallel version on the host, `PIPEPAR.TOP`. See also Tables 5.2 and 5.5.

4

Running occam programs on a network of transputers

We first need to explain something of the structure of the transputer to help understand the distribution of programs on a network of transputers. In Section 4.2, following the philosophy of presenting the simplest possible programs to illustrate the point in hand, we give a minimal program to show how to use a network. In it, the host sends a special signal to a second transputer and receives back a message indicating the network is alive and kicking. We return to placing the Newton-Raphson on a network in Chapter 5.

We also introduce some further occam: `PROC`s, `IF`s, `ALT`s, `PLACE`, `SC` and `PROGRAM`.

4.1 Structure of transputers

The transputer is a VLSI microcomputer with a processor, memory and four communication links (see Figure 4.1). There are several types of transputer, for example: T4 (32-bit word); T2 (16-bit); and T8 (32-bit incorporating a floating point unit). On the T4 internal memory is usually 2k bytes of RAM, and the 32-bit address/data bus allows up to 4 Gbytes of external memory. The processing speed is up to 10 MIPs (million instructions/sec).

Each link is connected to the main processor via a link interface allowing direct memory access. A transputer can communicate simultaneously on all four links, whilst executing an internal process. Each link implements two occam channels, one for input, the other for output, at speeds of 5, 10, or 20 million bits/sec in both directions simultaneously (depending on the setting of certain switches).

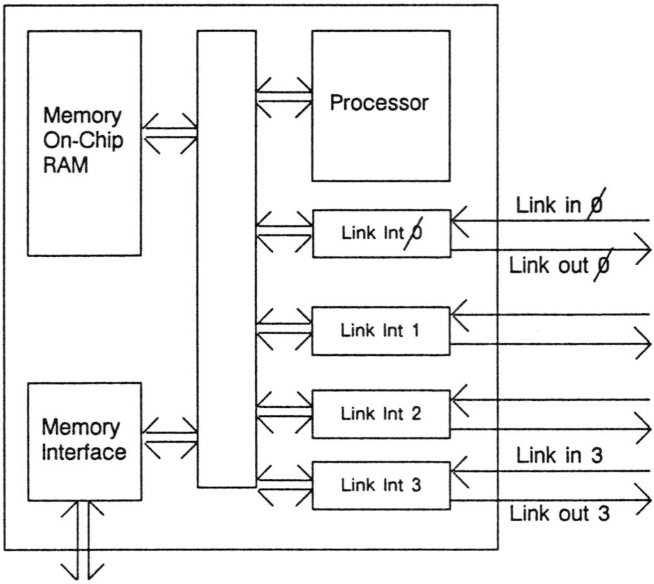

Figure 4.1 Transputer structure

One problem arising from only four links is that data passing between two widely separated transputers may need to be routed through others on the way – Chapter 6 shows how this can be achieved. In some cases, this also means the data must be tagged with the number of the destination transputer.

Figure 4.2 shows the link names and their addresses. `link1out,` for example, is a name chosen by INMOS convention to represent the output channel on link 1; the actual name is in fact optional but descriptive and you could choose any name you wish. In occam programs, link1out is defined as 1; this 1 is interpreted as hardware address #80000004 by the system, the address of the out channel of link 1. The host transputer connects to the IBM via link 0; link 2 is the default for connecting to a network.

4.1.1 Internal channels (soft channels)

These channels are within a single transputer and are not mapped onto links. Instead, when a channel is defined, a single word of storage is allocated. The two processes which are connected by the channels can access this word, when running. The first one to do so writes a "ready" signal into this word and is then suspended until the second process is ready to communicate. Transfer of data then occurs directly (i.e. not through any real channel) between the processes; the second process continues (it is never suspended), and the first joins the queue of other processes waiting to execute.

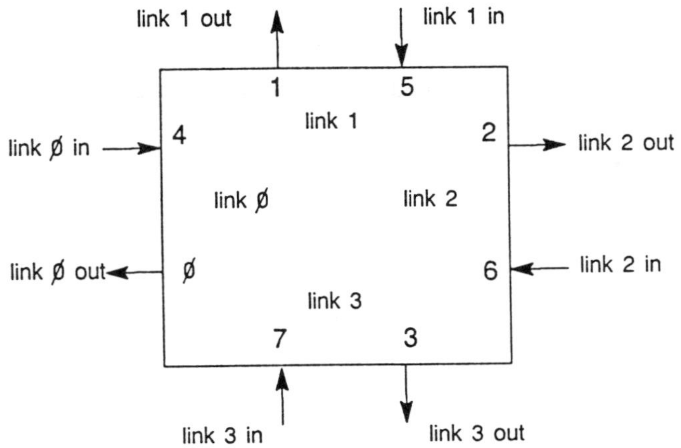

Figure 4.2 Link names and addresses

4.1.2 External channels (hard channels)

These are mapped onto the physical links (see Section 4.4). The link interfaces are responsible for descheduling the process, transferring the entire message (its length in bytes and the data itself) and then rescheduling the process. The transferred message is stored directly in the memory of the receiving transputer without interrupting its processor, thus allowing fast processing.

Two transputers can be linked by connecting them with two one-directional signal wires (see Section 4.5), along which data is transmitted serially. Each byte of the message must be acknowledged before the next is sent. A byte is transmitted as eleven bits: two leading ones, the eight bits of data and then a zero as a stop bit. The receiving transputer requires only a single-byte buffer, in the link interface, to ensure no information is lost.

4.2 A simple network program

Figure 4.3 shows the processes for a minimal program which demonstrates how to use a network (of the host and one T2 transputer). The Keyboard and Screen handler run on the host and communicate with the application, which will eventually run on the single T2. However, as indicated in Section 3.4, it is almost certainly quicker (even with a completed program print out before you) to first compile and run the program on the host before considering placing it on the network. This we shall do and then place it on the network in Sections 4.4 and 4.5.

The application is trivial: all key strokes are sent to it by the keyboard handler. The application watches out for a special character (the digit '2'), forwards it to the screen handler which then displays a message "hello! from T2". All other characters are ignored, with the exception of a special stop character ("@"), whose use is described below. Every key pressed is also sent directly to the screen handler for echoing on the screen.

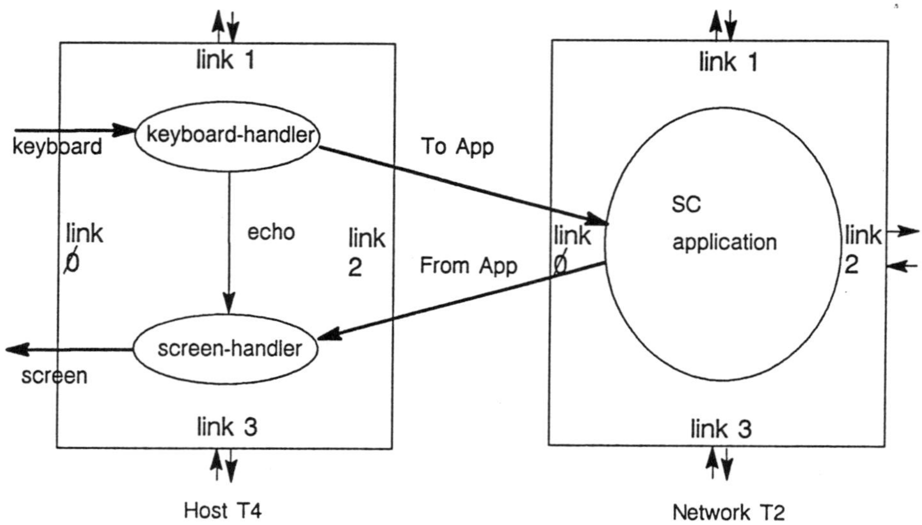

Figure 4.3 Processes for simple network program

We introduce the use of procedures (`PROC`), and the `IF` and `ALT` constructs in Section 4.3, and the idea of terminating processes.

4.3 Explanation of the program

Listings 4.1 to 4.5 show the folds containing the occam code for this program, called SIMPNET. The three processes (procedures) `Keyboard.handler`, `Screen.handler` and `Application` run in parallel. (see Listing 4.1).

Listing 4.1 is shown on the next page:

```
{{{F SIMPNET.TOP
... EXE Simple network program

}}}

{{{ EXE Simple network program
...F Simple network program
...F code
...F descriptor
...F link
...F debug
...F CODE EXE Simple network program
}}}

{{{F Simple network program

... Comments on prog

#USE userio

... CHANs

... PROC Keyboard.handler
... PROC Screen.handler
... PROC Application

PAR
  Keyboard.handler     (keyboard, To.App, echo)
  Screen.handler       (From.App, echo, screen)
  Application          (To.App, From.App)

}}}

{{{ Comments on prog
-- Accepts character from keyboard, and echoes to screen.
-- Also sends it on to an application, which watches out for
-- the ch. '2', and then send this on to the screen handler.
-- This version is for the host alone.
}}}

{{{ CHANs
CHAN OF INT To.App, From.App, echo:
}}}
```

Listing 4.1 The outer folds for the simple network program, developed for the host alone (SIMPNET)

4.3.1 Terminating parallel processes and deadlock

When several parallel processes are running, care must be exercised to ensure that they all stop running gracefully on completion of the program (graceful termination is not usually a major concern in a sequential program). If the processes do not communicate, for example, stopping one would leave all the others still running. If they do communicate, stopping one could lead to "deadlock", unless care is taken to stop all of them. Deadlock occurs in a set of processes when it is impossible for any of them to proceed; the effect on a running program is to seize it up, with nothing happening, save a blinking cursor (from the frequency with which it occurs, it might be better known as "dreadlock"!). For example, in Figure 4.4, process `P1` cannot send along `Chan1` until `P2` is ready to read; but `P2` cannot read, as it is waiting to send to `P1`.

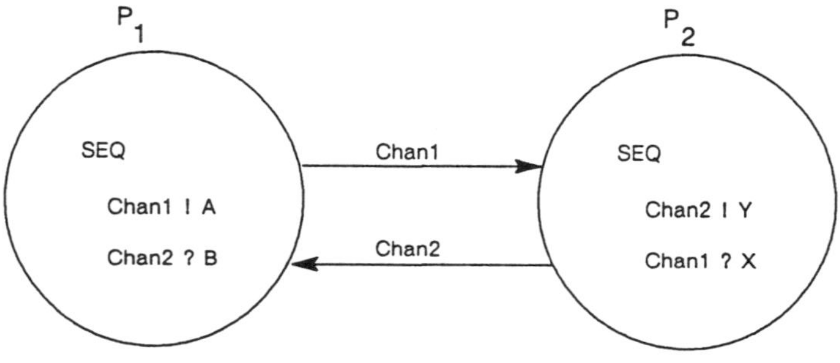

Figure 4.4 Deadlock

In occam, parallel processes are not allowed to share variables; consider, for example, what would happen if one process were allowed to read a variable that could be altered in another parallel process – which value would be read? Thus, a global flag to stop all parallel processes is ruled out. Instead, a "close down" message can be passed to all parallel processes. In our current example the message "stopch" is simply the character "@". Each of the three parallel processes continue operating while the Boolean variable `running` is `TRUE` (see Listings 4.2, 4.3 and 4.4). When the "@" key is pressed, the keyboard handler passes this on to the application and also to the screen handler. In each case, the finish Section responds to the "@" by setting `running` to `FALSE`. The `stopch` is defined by a `VAL` in each of the three processes.

```
{{{ PROC Keyboard.handler
PROC Keyboard.handler (CHAN OF INT keyboard,
                       CHAN OF INT To.App, echo)

  -- Accepts character input from keyboard and sends it on
  -- (i) to echo to screen and (ii) to the application.

  ... Declarations

  SEQ
    running := TRUE

    WHILE running
      SEQ
        keyboard ? ch

        PAR
          echo ! ch
          To.App ! ch

        ... finished ?
:
}}}

{{{ Declarations
INT ch:
VAL stopch IS INT '@':
BOOL running:
}}}

{{{ finished ?
IF
  ch = stopch
    running := FALSE
  ch <> stopch
    SKIP
}}}
```

Listing 4.2 The Keyboard handler PROC fold (SIMPNET and SIMPNET2)

4.3.2 PROC

A `PROC` (or, equivalently, procedure) is a named process whose body is terminated with a "`:`", in the same column as the "`P`" of `PROC`. The procedure parameters in this program are all of type `CHAN OF INT`. Examples of other types will be found in later chapters.

4.3.3 The IF constructor

This is different from the usual Pascal `IF`. In occam, `IF` takes any number of processes, each of which has a conditional test before it and makes them into a single process.

The `IF` process executes the first component whose condition is `TRUE` and then terminates. If all conditions are `FALSE`, then occam behaves like a `STOP`, a situation which may be hard to trace if it is inadvertent in a program.

Thus in Listing 4.2, if the character is not a "@", the `SKIP` simply does nothing and completes the `IF` construct in this case. Without the `SKIP`, the program would STOP whenever any key other than '@' were pressed. `TRUE` can be used as a condition, as a kind of "catch all" category – but beware! You must cater for all alternatives correctly if you use this (N.B. `ELSE` cannot be used with `IF` in occam).

Note the indentation after `IF`, and after each condition; and that `IF` is on a separate line.

4.3.4 ALT constructor

To see this in action, see Listing 4.3, the `Screen.handler` fold.

Sometimes a process needs to perform one of a number of actions depending on which input channel first sends its message. The `ALT`ernative constructor chooses just one of its inputs for execution, executes the corresponding process and then exits the `ALT` construct. The choice is done randomly if there are several ready channels when the `ALT` process is entered. If none of the inputs is ready, the `ALT` waits until one is. `ALT` is a selector on channels (unlike `IF`, which selects on conditions involving variables).

Thus in Listing 4.3, the `ALT` selects input either for echo from the `Key-board.handler` or from the `Application`, whichever happens to have a message to send. `ALT`s are usually embedded in a `WHILE` loop, so next time round another alternative may be selected.

Note that `ALT`s cannot select on output channels. This is not allowed in occam, since it could give rise to difficulties when output on one `ALT` process is connected via a channel to the input of another `ALT` process. However, the need to output to one or another channel does arise and Section 6.5 (in chapter 6) shows a way to achieve the effect.

```
{{{ PROC Screen.handler
PROC Screen.handler (CHAN OF INT From.App, echo,
                     CHAN OF ANY screen)

  -- Accepts input from either application or echo
  -- and sends to screen
  ... Declarations

  SEQ
    running := TRUE

    WHILE running
      ALT
        ... input from echo

        ... input from application
:
}}}

{{{ Declarations
INT ch:
BOOL running:
... VALs
}}}

{{{ input from echo
echo ? ch
  SEQ
    ... clear previous character
    ... print new character

    ... finished ?

}}}

{{{ input from application
From.App ? ch
  SEQ
    ... clear previous message
    ... print new message
}}}
```

Listing 4.3 The screen handler PROC fold (SIMPNET and SIMPNET2)

4.3.5 Writing to the screen

Listing 4.4 shows the folds for displaying the keys pressed on the screen. `write.char` and `goto.xy` are procedures in the library `userio`. `goto.xy (screen, echo.col, echo.row)` positions the cursor at position (10,5) on the screen; the constants are defined in the `VALs`.

```
{{{ VALs
VAL stopch     IS INT '@':
VAL app.row    IS 10:          -- position for application
VAL app.col    IS 5:           -- printing
VAL echo.row   IS 5:           -- position for echo printing
VAL echo.col   IS 5:
}}}

{{{ clear previous character
goto.xy (screen , echo.col, echo.row)
write.full.string (screen, "          ")
}}}

{{{ print new character
goto.xy (screen , echo.col, echo.row)
write.char (screen, BYTE ch)
}}}

{{{ finished ?
IF
  ch = stopch
    running := FALSE
  ch <> stopch
    SKIP
}}}

{{{ clear previous message
goto.xy (screen, app.col, app.row)
write.full.string (screen, "                        ")
}}}

{{{ print new message
goto.xy (screen, app.col, app.row)
write.char (screen, BYTE ch)
write.full.string (screen, "hello ! from Application")
}}}
```

Listing 4.4 The VALs, print and finish folds (SIMPNET and SIMPNET2)

```
{{{ PROC Application
PROC Application (CHAN OF INT To.App, From.App)

  -- Watches for the ch. '2' from keyboard handler and sends
  -- it on to screen handler. All other chars.
  -- (except stopch) are ignored.

  ... Declarations

  SEQ
    running := TRUE

    WHILE running
      SEQ

        To.App ? ch

        ... If a '2' send on to screen handler
        ... If a 'stopch' finish application
:
}}}

{{{ Declarations
BOOL running:
INT ch:
VAL To.App.ch      IS INT '2':
VAL stopch         IS INT '@':
}}}

{{{ If a '2' send on to screen handler
IF
  ch = To.App.ch
    From.App ! ch
  ch <> To.App.ch
    SKIP
}}}

{{{ If a 'stopch' finish application
IF
  ch = stopch
    running := FALSE
  ch <> stopch
    SKIP
}}}
```

Listing 4.5 The Application PROC fold (SIMPNET)

4.3.6 The Application

This is shown in Listing 4.5 on the previous page and is as described in Section 4.2.

At this stage, you should type in this program (Listings 4.1 to 4.5) and get it working on the Host before preparing it to run on the network. Allow approximately 30 minutes typing time.

4.4 Transforming the program to run on a network (of one transputer)

Listings 4.6 to 4.9 show the code for the same program to run on the host and one T2; there are several changes, though the code for the `PROC`s `Keyboard.handler` and `Screen.handler` are exactly the same as in Listings 4.2 to 4.4, and we do not repeat them here. The program is called SIMPNET2.

```
{{{F SIMPNET2.TOP
... EXE key and screen
... PROGRAM Application
}}}

{{{ EXE key and screen
...F key and screen
...F code
...F descriptor
...F link
...F debug
...F CODE EXE key and screen
}}}

{{{ PROGRAM Application
...F Application
...F code
...F descriptor
...F CODE PROGRAM Application
}}}
```

Listing 4.6 The outer folds for the simple network program, for host and one T2 (SIMPNET2)

First the `.TOP` fold has changed – the host code is in an `EXE` fold but the application has been removed and is now in a `PROGRAM` fold (created using the compilation unit key @7), indicating it is destined to run on the network.

```
{{{F key and screen
... Comments on program SIMPNET2

#USE userio

... hard channel placement values
... CHANs
... PLACEMENTS

... PROC Keyboard.handler
... PROC Screen.handler

PAR
  Keyboard.handler (keyboard, To.App, echo)
  Screen.handler   (From.App, echo, screen)
}}}

{{{ Comments on prog
-- Accepts character input from keyboard, and echoes it to
-- screen. Also sends it on to an application, which
-- watches out for the ch. '2', and then send this on to
-- the screen handler.

-- This version is for the host and one other transputer on
-- the network.
}}}

{{{ hard channel placement values
VAL link0out IS 0:
VAL link1out IS 1:
VAL link2out IS 2:
VAL link3out IS 3:
VAL link0in  IS 4:
VAL link1in  IS 5:
VAL link2in  IS 6:
VAL link3in  IS 7:
}}}

{{{ CHANs
CHAN OF INT To.App, From.App, echo:
}}}

{{{ PLACEMENTS
PLACE To.App   AT link2out:
PLACE From.App AT link2in:
}}}
```

Listing 4.7 The EXE key and screen folds running on the host (SIMPNET2)

4.4.1 Channel placements (allocation)

A major change is the association of channels with physical links, using PLACE statements. We selected link2 on the host to communicate with the T2, (this is the TDS default) via the channels To.App and From.App (Listing 4.7, PLACEMENTS fold):

```
PLACE To.App AT link2out:
```

associates the channel To.App with the physical link named link2out.

Each PLACE...AT... must be on a separate line; so, for example:

```
PLACE To.App AT link2out, From.App AT link2in:
```

is not allowed.

The values associated with link2out, link2in etc. follow the INMOS convention and are defined in the fold hard channel placement values; all link addresses are defined, though not all are used in this example. (It is easy to copy the entire fold whenever required).

Channel placement for the application in the PROGRAM on the T2 is shown in Listing 4.9. Again we have chosen to associate the name link0in with address 4 and PLACED the channel To.App at the physical link0in.

4.4.2 PROGRAM

The word "PROGRAM" signifies occam code that is to be run on a network, exclusive of the host. The application is now in a PROGRAM fold (Listings 4.6 and 4.8) and we have of necessity included the PROC Application in an SC (separately compiled) fold; all code that is to be loaded on a particular transputer must be wrapped up in an SC fold.

The application PROC is much as before, with the exception of the addition of the two folds hard channel placement values and PLACEMENTS (See Listing 4.9). The PROC Application is now called without channels To.App, From.App as parameters (compare Listing 4.1) since these are now PLACED within the SC. PLACED PAR in the Application fold of Listing 4.8 indicates the following processors run in parallel (there is only one in this case!; but see also Listing 5.4). PROCESSOR 1 T2 indicates that transputer 1 is of type T2; it is running the Application code. The choice of 1 here is just a logical identifier of that processor and may be any integer value; the actual value is of no significance, save to distinguish one processor from another.

```
{{{F Application
... SC PROC Application

PLACED PAR
  PROCESSOR 1 T2 -- change to T4 if required
    Application ()

}}}

{{{ SC PROC Application
...F PROC Application
...F code
...F descriptor
...F link
...F debug
}}}

{{{ PROC Application
PROC Application ()

   ... Comments on Proc

   ... Declarations

   SEQ
     running := TRUE

     WHILE running
       SEQ

         To.App ? ch

         ... If a '2' send on to screen handler
         ... If a 'stopch' finish application
:
}}}
```

Listing 4.8 The PROGRAM Application fold running on the T2 (SIMPNET2)

```
{{{ Comments on Proc
-- Watches for the ch. '2' from keyboard handler and sends
-- it on to screen handler. All other chars.
-- (except stopch) are ignored.

-- Note that INT32 must be used as the host T4 sends 32 bit
-- integers. This should not need changing if you are
-- using a T4 and not a T2.
}}}

{{{ Declarations
... VARs
... VALs
... hard channel placement values
... PLACEMENTS
}}}

{{{ VARs
BOOL running:
INT32 ch:        -- INT32 NECESSARY FOR A T2
}}}

{{{ VALs
VAL To.App.ch IS INT32 '2':       -- INT32 NECESSARY FOR A T2
VAL stopch    IS INT32 '@':
}}}

{{{ hard channel placement values
VAL link0out IS 0:
VAL link1out IS 1:
VAL link2out IS 2:
VAL link3out IS 3:
VAL link0in  IS 4:
VAL link1in  IS 5:
VAL link2in  IS 6:
VAL link3in  IS 7:
}}}

{{{ PLACEMENTS
CHAN OF INT32 To.App, From.App: -- INT32 NECESSARY FOR A T2

PLACE To.App   AT link0in:
PLACE From.App AT link0out:
}}}
```

Listing 4.9 Declaration and Placement folds for the Application on the T2 (SIMPNET2)

4.4.3 An important change

The literature seems to suggest that configuring does not affect the structure of occam code already working on a host; this must be qualified. In Listing 4.9 there is a critical change, in the VARs, VALs and PLACEMENTs folds: we have changed the INTs to INT32s, since, by default, on the host T4 INT is 32 bits and INT on a T2 is 16 bits. If this change is not made, deadlock will ensue when running with the network. The programs as written should however still function correctly with no changes if a T4 is used in place of the T2.

4.5 Running the program on the network

Type in the program by copying the one above (SIMPNET.TOP) into a new fold SIMPNET2.TOP and editing it into EXE and PROGRAM folds. The PROCs of the EXE (Keyboard and Screen.handler, Listings 4.2 to 4.4) do not need changing. (approximately 25 minutes typing time).

The EXE part is compiled for the T4 as before.

4.5.1 Preparing the *PROGRAM* fold for the network

Once the PROGRAM is created using the editor, it needs to be compiled for a T2 and then loaded onto the network. You must change the compiler parameter target.processor so that it compiles for a T2 and not a T4. You will find the compiler fold in the Toolkit fold (@F1).

With the cursor on the PROGRAM fold, @2 first compiles all the SCs within it. Extraction links all the code in the PROGRAM into a single CODE PROGRAM fold, which can then be loaded onto the network. Separate extraction (@3) is not obligatory, because loading the network (@4) also first extracts if necessary. However, the "results" are not saved in the fold and loading again on another occasion will entail extraction again. Thus separate extraction can save considerable time, for example, when reloading crashed programs during debugging.

You can also create a compilation information fold (@6), which is inserted inside the PROGRAM fold as CONFIG INFO PROGRAM Application. Figure 4.5 shows the results. The boot path gives the order in which booting of the transputers will occur; and the wiring diagram shows how to interconnect the network. In the present case, both these are rudimentary (see Section 5.3.2 for a fuller example).

```
{{{ Processor Load Map

{{{ Processor 1 T2
    Memory layout           first byte      last byte
Work space                  #81BA           #81CF
Main program                #81D0           #81DD
Real OP not loaded
SC PROC application         #81DE           #820F
No libraries loaded
}}}
}}}

{{{ Processor Boot Path
processor 1 from host
}}}

{{{ Wiring Diagram
Only one processor in network
}}}

}}}
```

Figure 4.5 CONFIG INFO PROGRAM Application Fold

Loading is by @4, but the network must already be connected correctly and powered up, otherwise clearly this can not be done (you will get an error message if you inadvertently try it).

In summary, to configure and load a program onto the network:

(i) change the compiler to compile to a T2 (@F1 for toolkit)

(ii) compile (@2) the PROGRAM fold

(iii) extract (to a file) @3

(iv) @4 to load the network (having made sure the wiring is correct and the board's power supply is on)

(v) create a compilation information fold @6 (if you want)

4.5.2 Wiring the network

Figures 4.6 to 4.8 show the layout of the edge connectors of the BOO4 and BOO6 boards, respectively. INMOS have made connecting the cable plugs to the sockets as foolproof as possible. For example, the 5-pin plugs will fit only one way round.

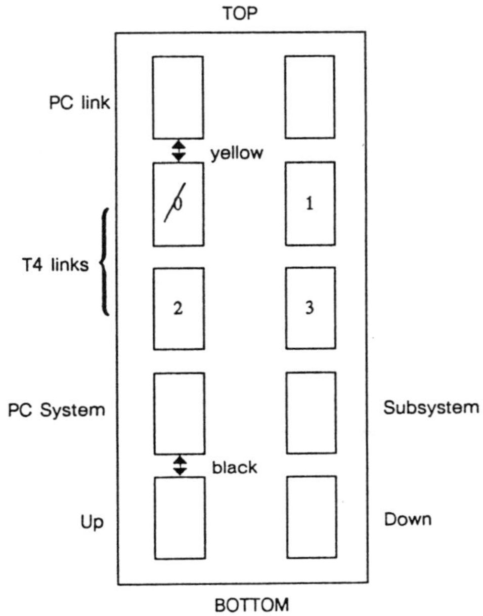

Figure 4.6 B004 edge connector

On the BOO4, at the back of the IBM PC, some connections are already in place to allow the host T4 to function with the IBM. Link0 of the T4 is connected by yellow cable to the PC bus via the socket "PClink"; this enables the keyboard and screen channels to function. "PCsystem" is connected to "Up" by a black cable. This allows communications and analysis of any transputer errors with the PC (for example, so the debugger can be used).

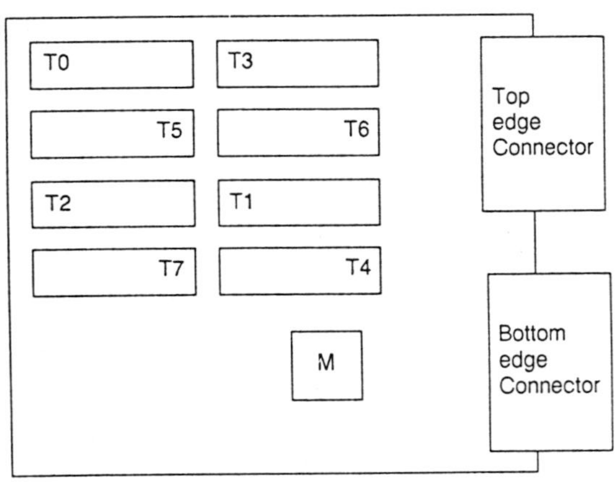

Figure 4.7 B006 board layout

To connect an additional board (i.e. not just an extra transputer; in our case the BOO6 board), the "Subsystem" socket is connected to the "Up" of the BOO6.

The BOO6 board layout is shown in Figure 4.7. M refers to the "Master" transputer which comes with the board.

There are 8 further positions, marked T0 to T7, for up to 8 further transputers. The lettering can be confusing especially when combined with "naming" of a processor such as PROCESSOR 1 T2, where the 1 does not necessarily refer to the position T1 on the board (any transputer could be designated 1). In fact, the numbering is even further confused by the first transputer being referred to as the master.

The positions T0 to T7 have several "hard-wired" link connections, forming two squares T0,T1,T2,T3 and T4,T5,T6,T7, using links 2 and 3 in each case. All other links are free to connect as you wish.

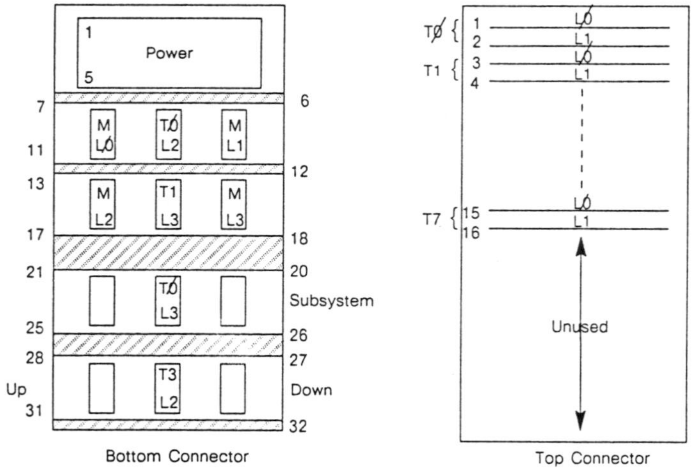

Figure 4.8 B006 bottom and top edge connectors

There are two edge connectors; the bottom one (see Figure 4.8) has 32 rows of pins, of which rows 1 to 5 are used for the power supply. Some are not used and are either sleeved or cut short. (Rows 6, 12,18,19,20,26,27,32). The socket marked M L0 (rows 7 to 11, left-hand side) refers to the link0 of the master transputer; T3 L2 (rows 28 to 31, middle) refers to the transputer in position T3, link2; and so on.

The BOO4 host board is connected to the "Up" socket of the BOO6; "Subsystem" and "Down" can be used for connecting further boards.

The top edge connector is used for connecting links 0 and 1 of each of T0 through T7. Again there are 32 rows, of 3 pins, but only the first 16 are connected. There are two rows for each transputer in turn (T0 to T7); the first row is for `link0` and the second for `link1`.

To connect for the above program ensure:

(i) "Subsystem" of BOO4 connected to "Up" of B006 using long (2m) reset cable (grey strip).

(ii) link2 of BOO4 connected to ML0 of B006 using long (2m) link cable (2 twisted pairs).

4.5.3 Running the program

Having compiled the `EXE` and `PROGRAM` folds, and switched on the network:

(i) Load the `PROGRAM` as described in Section 4.5.1

(ii) Load the `EXE` as usual (F5)

(iii) Run by using F6

To rerun the program, you must first reload the network; do not load and run the `EXE` before you have loaded the network, otherwise you will experience deadlock.

5

Preparing the Newton-Raphson program for the network

5.1 Introduction

We now turn to writing the Newton-Raphson program on a network of several transputers (i.e. more than one in the network).

We arrange for the total number of iterations `N` to be shared as equally as possible amongst the `M` transputers in the network (excluding the host). For example, if we wanted 13 iterations on five transputers, rather than have two iterations on the five transputers with the remaining three added to the last, a better balance is three on each of the first three transputers and two iterations on each of the last two. In the first case, the speed of the pipeline would be reduced to that of the five iterations on the last processor.

In general we want each of the first (`N REM M`) transputers to do (`N DIV M + 1`) iterations, and each of the remainder (`N DIV M`). (`DIV` is integer divide, truncated, and `REM` is remainder modulo `M`).

Figure 5.1 shows how the occam code is distributed on four transputers, and the links used. There is the host T4, with three T2 transputers in the network.

The host runs an `EXE` which generates the integers and feeds them to the network (via `link2` of the T4); in parallel, a second process bleeds the pipeline (via `link3`) and sends the results to display on the screen.

Each of the transputers in the network runs the `SC` process which performs several iterations, as described above. On each one , `link0` receives the incoming data (`x, est`) and `link1` passes it on to the next processor. `Link2` of the host is thus connected to `link0` of Processor 1 and `link1` of Processor 3 to `link3` of the host.

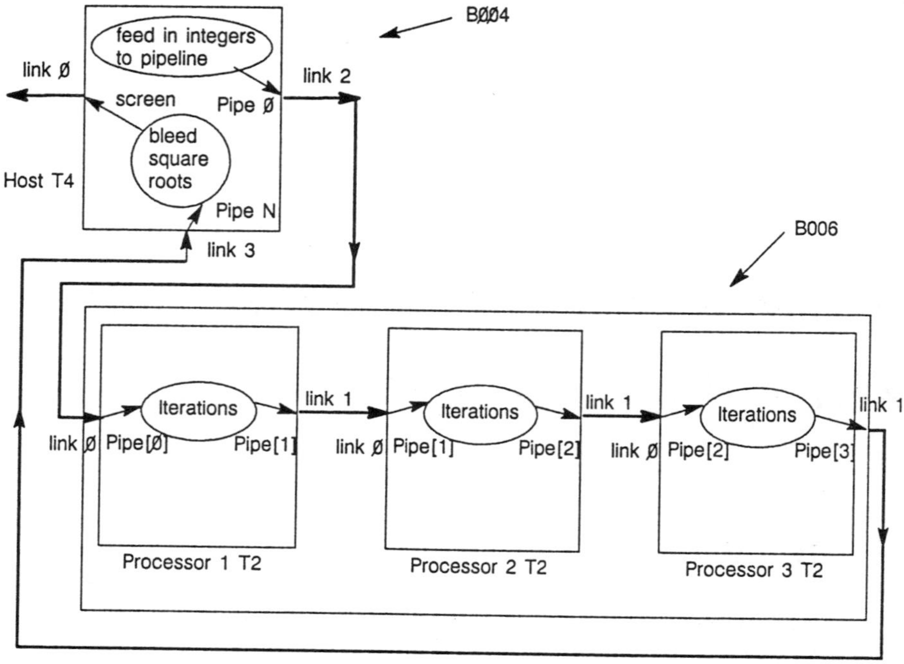

Figure 5.1 Host + Network: code distribution

5.2 Explanation of program PARMN

Listing 5.1 on the next page shows the top-level folds for this program.

5.2.1 The EXE fold (on the host)

Listing 5.2 (also on the next page) shows the main part of the `EXE` fold. Compare this with Listings 3.4 to 3.7.

```
{{{F PARMN.TOP
... EXE feedmn and bleed
... PROGRAM parmn

}}}

{{{ EXE feedmn and bleed
...F feedmn and bleed
...F code
...F descriptor
...F link
...F debug
...F CODE EXE feedmn and bleed
}}}

{{{ PROGRAM parmn
...F parmn
...F code
...F descriptor
...F CODE PROGRAM parmn
}}}
```

Listing 5.1 Top-level folds for Newton-Raphson program on a network (PARMN)

Start of Listing 5.2:

```
{{{F feedmn and bleed

#USE userio
... Comments on program

PROC feed.bleed ()
  ... hard channel placement values
  ... CHANs and PROTOCOL
  ... PLACEMENTS
  ... VALs etc
  ... main feed and bleed program

:

... running
... feed and bleed
... finished and pause
}}}
```

Listing 5.2: page two

```
{{{ Comments on program
-- Runs on the B004.

-- Program starts up and then feeds the pipeline running
-- on a B006 and also bleeds the pipeline for displaying
-- results if required.

-- Newton-Raphson program for extracting the square roots
-- of the first R integers. Parallel program for host
-- transputer + M T2 transputers on the B006.

-- N is the number of iterations to be used.
-- R is the number of square roots to be extracted
}}}

{{{ hard channel placement values
VAL link0out IS 0:
VAL link1out IS 1:
VAL link2out IS 2:
VAL link3out IS 3:
VAL link0in  IS 4:
VAL link1in  IS 5:
VAL link2in  IS 6:
VAL link3in  IS 7:
}}}

{{{ CHANs and PROTOCOL
PROTOCOL x.est IS REAL32; REAL32:
CHAN OF x.est Pipe0, PipeN:
}}}

{{{ PLACEMENTS
PLACE Pipe0 AT link2out:
PLACE PipeN AT link3in:
}}}

{{{ VALs etc
VAL Half IS 0.5 (REAL32):
VAL R IS 5:
}}}
```

Listing 5.2: page three

```
{{{ running
INT Any:
SEQ
  write.full.string (screen, "Started running --")
  newline (screen)
  keyboard ? Any
}}}

{{{ feed and bleed
  feed.bleed ()
}}}

{{{ finished and pause
  write.full.string (screen, "Finished running -- ")
  keyboard ? Any

}}}
```

Listing 5.2 Main part of EXE fold – the feed and bleed for Newton-Raphson program (PARMN)

We note the following changes:

Code moved to *PROGRAM*

All the code for the iterations is now in the `PROGRAM`. Thus, `N` is no longer in `VALs` and in the `main feed and bleed program` fold (see Listing 5.3) we have removed the `main pipeline` fold. The definition of the `N+1` channels of `Pipe` has also been transferred.

Other changes

In the `CHANS and PROTOCOL` fold we have defined `Pipe0` and `PipeN` (we can no longer use `Pipe[0]` and `Pipe[N]`) and `PLACED` them at `link2out` and `link3in`, respectively.

`Pipe0` and `PipeN` also replace `Pipe[0]` and `Pipe[N]` in Listing 5.3 in the folds `feed in integers`, and `bleed square roots`; otherwise these folds are the same as before.

```
{{{ main feed and bleed program
PAR
  ... feed in integers to pipeline
  ... bleed square roots

}}}

{{{ feed in integers to pipeline
SEQ r = 1 FOR R
  REAL32 x, est:
  SEQ
    x   := (REAL32 ROUND r)
    est := x * Half
    Pipe0 ! x; est
}}}

{{{ bleed square roots
SEQ r = 1 FOR R
  REAL32 x, est:
  SEQ
    PipeN ? x; est
    ... print square roots

}}}

{{{ print square roots
... VALs
SEQ
  write.full.string (screen, "x = ")
  write.real32 (screen, x, Ip, Dp)
  write.full.string (screen, "sqrt(x) = ")
  write.real32 (screen, est, Ip, Dp)
  newline (screen)

}}}

{{{ VALs
VAL Ip IS 5:
VAL Dp IS 3:
}}}
```

Listing 5.3 The main feed and bleed fold (PARMN)

5.2.2 The *PROGRAM* fold (on the network (B006))

The details of the PROGRAM fold are in Listing 5.4 There are M transputers in the network, so:

```
PLACED PAR m = 1 FOR M
```

places the "Iterations" code on each processor m, to run concurrently with all the others. (Again m is an arbitrary reference number). Pipe[m-1] and Pipe[m] are placed at link0in, link1out of the corresponding transputer as m changes from 1 to M. We placed Pipe0 at link2out of the host T4 and this matches up with Pipe[0] of processor 1 of the network.

Finally, note that the iterations code depends through its parameter list on the transputer number m. M is also passed as a parameter (this is so that we can detect the last transputer in the pipeline and thus send the final x,est back to the host, instead of passing them on to the "next" in the pipeline; see Figure 5.1). Note that M is defined as a constant (in the VALs fold). By passing it as a parameter, we avoid redefining M as a constant within the SC process Iterations. A VAL parameter (see Listing 5.5) indicates that the value of the parameter is constant within the procedure and thus must not be assigned to. A parameter without a VAL is passed by reference (its value can be changed in the procedure), and is similar to VAR parameters in Pascal.

Start of Listing 5.4:

```
{{{F parmn
... Comments on program

PROTOCOL x.est IS REAL32; REAL32:

... SC Iterations

... hard channel placement values
... VALs
... CHANS
PLACED PAR m = 1 FOR M
  PROCESSOR m T2                    --CHANGE TO T4
  PLACE Pipe[m-1] AT link0in:        --IF REQUIRED
  PLACE Pipe[m] AT link1out:
  Iterations (Pipe[m-1], Pipe[m], m, M)

}}}
```

```
{{{ Comments on program
-- Runs on the B006.

-- A Newton-Raphson program for extracting the square
-- roots of the first R integers. Parallel program
-- for host transputer + M T2 transputers on the B006.

-- N is the number of iterations to be used.
-- R is the number of square roots to be extracted
}}}

{{{ hard channel placement values
VAL link0out IS 0:
VAL link1out IS 1:
VAL link2out IS 2:
VAL link3out IS 3:
VAL link0in  IS 4:
VAL link1in  IS 5:
VAL link2in  IS 6:
VAL link3in  IS 7:
}}}

{{{ VALs
VAL M IS 3: -- Number of transputers in pipeline
}}}

{{{ CHANS
[M+1] CHAN OF x.est Pipe:
}}}
```

Listing 5.4 The PROGRAM fold (PARMN)

Again we have had to incorporate the `PROC` which is placed on the processors in an `SC`. The `PROTOCOL` is introduced in two places: at the start of the `parmn` fold so that `CHANS` fold can define `Pipe` (see Listing 5.4); and in the `SC` so that it can also define channels of `Input, Output` as `x.est` (see `Iterations` fold in Listing 5.5). Remember that there is a barrier between an `SC` and the outside world – information can only be transferred to an `SC` through the parameter list or a `PROTOCOL` in this fashion.

```
{{{ SC Iterations
... Iterations
}}}

{{{ Iterations
PROTOCOL x.est IS REAL32; REAL32:

PROC Iterations (CHAN OF x.est Input, Output,
                     VAL INT m, M)
  ... main pipeline
:
}}}

{{{ main pipeline
... VALs etc
... Number of iterations on each transputer

  SEQ r = 1 FOR R
    REAL32 x, est:

    SEQ
      Input ? x; est

      SEQ itno = 1 FOR N.Its
        est := ((est + (x/est)) * Half)
      Output ! x; est
}}}

{{{ VALs etc
VAL Half IS 0.5 (REAL32):
VAL R IS 5:  -- No. of Integers
VAL N IS 10: -- No. of iterations
}}}
```

Listing 5.5 The Iterations fold (PARMN)

In the `main pipeline` fold of Listing 5.5, we have removed:

```
PAR n = 1 FOR N
```

This is now, of course, the `PLACED PAR m = 1 FOR M`, in Listing 5.4. We have replaced `N` with `M`, and each transputer carries out several iterations, as discussed in Section 5.1. The code for this is in the fold `number of iterations on each transputer`, shown in Listing 5.6.

```
{{{ Number of iterations on each transputer

-- The total number of iterations is shared as
-- equally as possible amongst the M transputers
-- (ie Nm = N DIV M on each).
-- However, there will be (N REM M) iterations left
-- over; one iteration is given to each of the first
-- (N REM M) transputers.

INT Nm, N.Its:
SEQ
  Nm := N/M
  IF
    ... first N REM M transputers
    ... the others

}}}

{{{ first N REM M transputers
m <= (N REM M)
  N.Its := Nm + 1
}}}

{{{ the others
TRUE
  N.Its := Nm
}}}
```

Listing 5.6 Number of iterations on each transputer fold (PARMN)

The iterations proper are unchanged, with the exception of the addition of

```
SEQ itno = 1 FOR N.Its
```

to perform `N.Its` iterations on this transputer.

Input and `Output` are now defined in the parameter list of the `Iterations PROC`. Note that we have also to redefine the `VALs` for `Half` and `R`, for use here.

5.3 Running the Newton-Raphson program on the network

This procedure is similar to that described in Section 4.5. The `EXE` is compiled and linked for a T4; the program configured for a T2 network.

5.3.1 The configuration information for PROGRAM PARMN

The configuration information code for the PROGRAM is given in Figure 5.2. It consists of three main parts:

- ❑ the Processor Load Map for each transputer in the network
- ❑ the Processor Boot Path
- ❑ the Wiring Diagram

The Processor Load Map shows, for each transputer in the network, its number as given in the `PLACED PAR` process in Listing 5.4 and its type. These are followed by the memory addresses (in hexadecimal) of the various parts of the program. These are:

- ❑ the work space, or the scalar variable storage;
- ❑ the main program code;
- ❑ real OP code
- ❑ the code for SC procedures
- ❑ the code linked in from libraries
- ❑ the vector workspace, or array storage

For example, for the PARMN code the work space is from #8032 to #80B3 for each transputer (they each are running the same code). Because there is no real output, this memory address range is left blank.

5.3.2 Rearranging physical links

The cables linking the transputers need to be modified since the layout is now different from that of the example of Chapter 4. The configuration information in Figure 5.2 also shows the wiring diagram for each transputer. For example, link1 of processor 1 must be connected to link0 of processor 2; and link1 of processor 2 must be connected to link0 of processor 3.

However, since the host is not part of the network, the configuration information does not show that link1 of processor 3 must be connected to link3 of the host (see the `PLACEMENTS` fold in Listing 5.2) for the return of the computed square roots.

```
{{{ CONFIG INFO PROGRAM parmnread

{{{ Processor Load Map

{{{ Processor   1   T2
     Memory layout              first byte       last byte
Work space                      #8032            #80B3
Main program                    #80B4            #80C5
Real OP not loaded
SC Iterations                   #80C6            #8185
Libraries                       #8186            #87D1
No separate vector workspace
}}}

{{{ Processor   2   T2
     Memory layout              first byte       last byte
Work space                      #8032            #80B3
Main program                    #80B4            #80C5
Real OP not loaded
SC Iterations                   #80C6            #8185
Libraries                       #8186            #87D1
No separate vector workspace
}}}

{{{ Processor 3 T2
     Memory layout              first byte       last byte
Work space                      #8032            #80B3
Main program                    #80B4            #80C5
Real OP not loaded
SC Iterations                   #80C6            #8185
Libraries                       #8186            #87D1
No separate vector workspace
}}}
}}}
{{{ Processor Boot Path
processor 1 from host
processor 2 from processor 1 link 1
processor 3 from processor 2 link 1
}}}

{{{ Wiring Diagram
Connect processor 1 link 1 to processor 2 link 0
Connect processor 2 link 1 to processor 3 link 0
}}}
}}}
```

Figure 5.2 Configuration Information Fold for Newton-Raphson program (PARMN)

5.4 Reading in *R* and *N* – sending different data types down a channel

This Section illustrates the use of `CASE` with `PROTOCOLs`, for sending data of different types down the same channel. We modify the program to read in `R` and `N` from the keyboard initially and send them to each of the transputers in the net in turn, before starting the iterations proper. This avoids the tedious recompilation that we have used so far when running the programs for various values of `R` and `N`. Similarly, it would be desirable to read in the value of `M`, to vary the number of transputers; however, replicated `PARs` cannot have variable counts, so `M` must be changed manually followed by a recompilation. This is so that the compiler can know how many processes there are in a program, so that memory allocation can be done prior to execution.

Further, in defining channels (see `CHANs` fold in Listing 5.10) the array index must again be determinable at compile time. Listings 5.7 to 5.12 show the code needed. The outer folds (Listing 5.7) are similar to ones seen previously. This program is called `PARREAD`.

```
{{{F PARREAD.TOP
... EXE feedmnread and bleed
... PROGRAM parmnread

}}}

{{{ EXE feedmnread and bleed
...F feedmnread and bleed
...F code
...F descriptor
...F link
...F debug
...F CODE EXE feedmnread and bleed
}}}

{{{ PROGRAM parmnread
...F parmnread
...F code
...F descriptor
...F CODE PROGRAM parmnread
...F CONFIG INFO PROGRAM parmnread
}}}
```

Listing 5.7 Outer folds for Newton-Raphson program, which reads R and N initially (PARREAD)

5.4.1 Changes to the *EXE*

The changes to the EXE fold are as follows:

Variant *PROTOCOL*

The first change occurs in the `CHANs and PROTOCOL` fold of Listing 5.8, where we have used a `CASE` to define variant `PROTOCOLs`: the `NR` is for sending `N` and `R`, two 16-bit `INTs`. `R` and `N` are used on the T2s as `counts` in replicated `SEQs` and by default these must be of type `INT` i.e. 16-bit integers. `x.est` is as before. Thus, the `PROTOCOL comms` has two variants; it will accept either two 16-bit integers or two 32-bit reals. `R` and `N`, of course, have now been removed from the `VALs` fold.

Start of Listing 5.8:

```
{{{F feedmnread and bleed

#USE userio
... Comments on program
PROC feed.bleed ()
  ... hard channel placement values
  ... CHANs and PROTOCOL
  ... PLACEMENTS
  ... VALs etc
  ... main feed and bleed program

:

... running
... feed and bleed
... finished and pause
}}}

{{{ Comments on program
-- Runs on the B004.

-- Program starts up and then feeds the pipeline running
-- on a B006 and also bleeds the pipeline for displaying
-- results if required.

-- Newton-Raphson program for extracting the square roots
-- of the first R integers. Parallel program for host
-- transputer + M T2 transputers on the B006.
```

Listing 5.8: page two

```
-- N is the number of iterations to be used.
-- R is the number of square roots to be extracted

-- R, N are input from keyboard and passed to the network.
}}}

{{{ hard channel placement values
VAL link0out IS 0:
VAL link1out IS 1:
VAL link2out IS 2:
VAL link3out IS 3:
VAL link0in  IS 4:
VAL link1in  IS 5:
VAL link2in  IS 6:
VAL link3in  IS 7:
}}}

{{{ CHANs and PROTOCOL
PROTOCOL comms
  CASE
    NR ; INT16; INT16        -- send 16-bits INTs to the
    x.est ; REAL32; REAL32 --network
:

CHAN OF comms Pipe0, PipeN:
}}}

{{{ PLACEMENTS
PLACE Pipe0 AT link2out:
PLACE PipeN AT link3in:
}}}

{{{ VALs etc
VAL Half IS 0.5 (REAL32):
}}}
```

```
{{{ main feed and bleed program
... VARs

SEQ
  ... Read in R, N
  ... Send N, R to B006

  PAR
    ... feed in integers to pipeline
    ... bleed square roots
}}}

{{{ running
INT Any:
SEQ
  write.full.string (screen, "Started running --")
  newline (screen)
  keyboard ? Any
}}}

{{{ feed and bleed
  feed.bleed ()
}}}

{{{ finished and pause
  write.full.string (screen, "Finished running -- ")
  keyboard ? Any
}}}
```

Listing 5.8 Main part of EXE fold – the feed and bleed for Newton-Raphson program, which reads R and N initially (PARREAD)

Reading and echoing values

The main `EXE` fold now includes folds for reading `R` and `N` and sending them to the network before starting the Newton-Raphson iterations proper (see Listing 5.8 and 5.9). Since `read.echo.int` (in `read N` and `read R`) expect 32-bit integers as input (on a T4) we have defined the values input as 32-bits and then converted them to 16-bits before sending them to the network (see `send N,R to B006`); `error` is an error flag which must be set to zero before calling the read procedure. `read.echo.int` is contained in the library `USERIO`.

Start of Listing 5.9:

```
{{{ VARs
INT R32, N32:          -- 32 bit INTs read in from keyboard
INT16 R, N:            -- and converted to 16 bits to send
                       -- to B006
INT error:             -- used in inputting reals
}}}

{{{ Read in R, N
error := 0
... read N
... read R
}}}

{{{ read N
write.full.string (screen, "Type number of iterations N")
newline (screen)
read.echo.int (keyboard, screen, N32, error)
}}}

{{{ read R
write.full.string (screen, "Type number of integers R")
newline (screen)
read.echo.int (keyboard, screen, R32, error)
}}}

{{{ Send N, R to B006
N := INT16 (N32)
R := INT16 (R32)

Pipe0 ! NR; N; R
}}}

{{{ feed in integers to pipeline
SEQ r = 1 FOR R32
  REAL32 x, est:
  SEQ
    x   := (REAL32 ROUND r)
    est := x * Half
    Pipe0 ! x.est; x; est
}}}
```

```
{{{ bleed square roots
  SEQ r = 1 FOR R32
    REAL32 x, est:
    SEQ
      PipeN ? CASE x.est; x; est
      ... print square roots
}}}

{{{ print square roots
... VALs
SEQ
  write.full.string (screen, "x = ")
  write.real32 (screen, x, Ip, Dp)
  write.full.string (screen, "sqrt(x) = ")
  write.real32 (screen, est, Ip, Dp)
  newline (screen)
}}}

{{{ VALs
VAL Ip IS 5:
VAL Dp IS 3:
}}}
```

Listing 5.9 The main feed and bleed folds (PARREAD)

Outputting using variant *PROTOCOLS*

In `feed in integers` in Listing 5.9, the variables `x; est` are preceded by the `PROTOCOL` variant `x.est` to define the type of data package sent down the channel `Pipe0`.

Inputting using variant *PROTOCOLs*

In `bleed square roots` (Listing 5.9) we input from the B006; the name of the variant `PROTOCOL` above is not sufficient – `CASE` must be used. This is because the receiving process cannot know the type of incoming data and so must have a collection of possible read actions, one for each type of variant defined in the `PROTOCOL`. In the present situation the `CASE` is a shortened form, which is allowed if there is only one type of input. See the examples in Chapter 6 for more general `CASEs`.

5.4.2 Changes to the *PROGRAM*

Again, the `PROTOCOL` definitions incorporate the `CASE` statements, (Listings 5.10 and 5.11). The `Pipes` are now defined as `CHAN OF comms` in the `CHANs` fold, which allows for data transfer of either of the two variants `NR` or `x.est`.

Start of Listing 5.10:

```
{{{F parmnread
... Comments on program
... PROTOCOL

... SC Iterations

... hard channel placement values
... VALs
... CHANS

PLACED PAR m = 1 FOR M
  PROCESSOR m T2                  -- CHANGE TO T4
    PLACE Pipe[m-1] AT link0in:-- IF REQUIRED
    PLACE Pipe[m] AT link1out:
    Iterations (Pipe[m-1], Pipe[m], m, M)
}}}

{{{ Comments on program
-- Runs on the B006.

-- Newton-Raphson program for extracting square roots of
-- the first R integers. Parallel program for host
-- transputer + M T2 transputers on the B006.

-- N is the number of iterations to be used.
-- R is the number of square roots to be extracted

-- N, R are input through the channel "input"
}}}

{{{ PROTOCOL
PROTOCOL comms
  CASE
    NR ; INT; INT
    x.est ; REAL32; REAL32
:
}}}
```

```
{{{ hard channel placement values
VAL link0out IS 0:
VAL link1out IS 1:
VAL link2out IS 2:
VAL link3out IS 3:
VAL link0in  IS 4:
VAL link1in  IS 5:
VAL link2in  IS 6:
VAL link3in  IS 7:
}}}

{{{ VALs
VAL M IS 3:    -- 2 | 3 |
               -- Number of transputers in pipeline
}}}

{{{ CHANS
[M+1] CHAN OF comms Pipe:
}}}
```

Listing 5.10 The PROGRAM fold (PARREAD)

The main part of the iterations (Listing 5.11) now input `N` and `R` from the previous transputers before starting the iterations.

First part of Listing 5.11:

```
{{{ SC Iterations
... Iterations
}}}

{{{ Iterations
... PROTOCOL
PROC Iterations (CHAN OF comms Input, Output, VAL INT m, M)
  ... main pipeline
:
}}}

{{{ PROTOCOL
PROTOCOL comms
  CASE
    NR ; INT; INT
    x.est ; REAL32; REAL32
:
}}}
```

```
{{{ main pipeline
... VAR
... VALs etc
SEQ
  ... Input N and R and send on if not last transputer
  ... Number of iterations on each transputer

    SEQ r = 1 FOR R
      REAL32 x, est:

      SEQ
        Input ? CASE x.est; x; est

        SEQ itno = 1 FOR N.Its
          est := ((est + (x/est)) * Half)

        Output ! x.est; x; est
}}}
```

Listing 5.11 The Iterations fold (PARREAD)

Since N and R are no longer constants, we have removed them from the VALs fold (Listing 5.12) and declared them in the VAR fold (by implication they will be 16-bit INTs on the T2s). Again, outputting using variant protocols requires the tag field (x.est); and inputting, CASE along with the tag.

These are the only changes here.

Start of Listing 5.12:

```
{{{ VAR
INT N, R:
}}}

{{{ VALs etc
VAL Half IS 0.5 (REAL32):
}}}
```

```
{{{ Input N and R and send on if not last transputer
-- Receive number of iterations and integers

Input ? CASE NR; N; R

-- Send to next transputer if not the last one
IF
  m < M
    Output ! NR; N; R
  TRUE
    SKIP
}}}

{{{ Number of iterations on each transputer

-- The total number of iterations is shared as equally as
-- possible amongst the M transputers
-- (ie Nm = N DIV M on each).
-- However, there will be (N REM M) iterations left over; one
-- iteration is given to each of the first (N REM M)
-- transputers.

INT Nm, N.Its:
SEQ
  Nm := N/M
  IF
    ... first N REM M transputers
    ... the others
}}}

{{{ first N REM M transputers
m <= (N REM M)
  N.Its := Nm + 1
}}}

{{{ the others
TRUE
  N.Its := Nm
}}}
```

Listing 5.12 VAR, VALs and Number of Iterations fold (PARREAD)

5.5 Running on the network

This procedure is again similar to that described in Section 4.5, and the arrangement of the links as in Section 5.3.2. In this case, of course, values for `R` and `N` are read in from the keyboard, and the program can easily be rerun without recompilation or reconfiguration (but remember to reload the network each time).

5.5.1 Running with a different number of transputers, *M*

This requires changing the values of `M` in the `PROGRAM` in the `VALs` fold shown in Listing 5.10, followed by recompiling and reconfiguring. Before loading and running, the physical wiring must also be changed; for example, if M = 2, the T4 input link3in should be reconnected to the second T2 via its link1.

5.6 Speed, speed up and efficiency

You can now demonstrate the speed of a network of transputers compared with that of the IBM Micro, and also investigate how speed-up and efficiency depend on the number of transputers in a network.

Table 5.1 compares the speeds of two microcomputers (the IBM XT and Zenith Z-286) and a main frame VAX 8530; the micros were run with and without maths co-processors. 20000 integers were processed for 80 Newton-Raphson iterations (This would give approximately 10^{24} decimal place accuracy, if multi-length arithmetic were used! The point of so many iterations is to give a substantial computation load compared to communications – see Section 5.7 below.)

Table 5.1 Square root extraction for 20000 integers and 80 iterations on IBM, Zenith and VAX computers

	Without Co-processor		***With Co-processor***	
Processor	*Time (Secs)*	*MFlops*	*Time (Secs)*	*MFlops*
IBM XT (8088 + 8087)	3,000	0.0016	310	0.015
Zenith Z-286 (80286 + 80287)	1,260	0.0038	240	0.020
VAX 8530	- -	- -	7	0.68

The table shows the time in seconds for the processing, along with the "MFlops" obtained i.e. the number of mega (10^6) floating point operations per second. Flops are not regarded as a reliable indicator of processor performance, but are usually fairly easily measurable. In this case, we see from Section 3.1 that there are 3 floating point operations per iteration (an add, divide and multiply), or 6 x 10^4 operations/iteration for 20000 integers. For comparison, Table 5.2 shows the results obtained using the host T4 alone (no network) running the programs "PIPESEQ" and "PIPEPAR" of Chapter 3, with the number of iterations varying from 5 to 80. Note the considerable slow down of the PAR program due to the overhead of handling PARs on a single transputer.

Table 5.2 Square root extraction for 20000 integers using sequential and parallel Newton-Raphson on Host Transputer

Number of Iterations	**"PIPESEQ" SEQ**		**"PIPEPAR" PAR**	
N	*Time (Secs)*	*MFlops*	*Time (Secs)*	*MFlops*
5	5.2	0.059	6.18	0.048
10	9.4	0.064	11.63	0.052
20	18.2	0.066	31.11	0.039
40	36.0	0.067	73.0	0.033
80	72.0	0.067	158.0	0.030

Also, for the SEQ program, there is a nearly linear increase in time with the number of iterations N and (eventually) a constant value of MFlops. In the PAR case, the MFlops behave in a peculiar fashion. This will be explained in the next Section.

Table 5.3 Square root extraction for 20000 integers using networks of 1, 2 and 3 T2 transputers (Program PARMNREAD). E is efficiency

Number of Iterations	**1 Transputer**		**2 Transputers**			**3 Transputers**		
N	*Time (Secs)*	*MFlops*	*Time*	*MFlops (Secs)*	*E*	*Time (Secs)*	*MFlops*	*E*
5	13.3	0.022	8.4	0.036	79	6.0	0.050	74
10	25.4	0.023	13.3	0.045	95	10.8	0.055	78
20	49.3	0.024	25.3	0.047	97	18.0	0.067	91
40	97.2	0.025	49.3	0.049	98	34.9	0.069	93
80	193.4	0.025	97.5	0.049	99	66.2	0.073	97

Table 5.3 shows the effect of distributing the iterations over networks of one, two and three T2 transputers (we are limited to three T2s as that is all we have!). Efficiency is a measure of the utilisation of the transputers in the network and is defined as:

$E = T_1/(M \times T_M)$

where T_1 is the time the program takes on one transputer, and T_M the time taken when run on a network of M transputers. (The usual definition of efficiency would include 4 transputers here – the host + 3 in the network; however, since they are of different types and the host's contribution is relatively trivial, we have put M = 3). The MFlops increases with the number of iterations. Notice, also, that the efficiency decreases when 3 processors are used, although the performance, in terms of MFlops, increases. This results from the interplay between the ratio of computation and communication, as we shall see in the next Section.

5.7 Estimation of computation and communication times

By using the data published by INMOS (an extract is given in Table 5.4) we can obtain some ball-park figures for the computation and communication times for the Newton-Raphson programs. Most of the computation times are dominated (on T2s and T4s, at any rate) by the floating point arithmetic, in the nested replication loops. "Cycles" refers to processor cycles.

The floating point computation is done by software on the 16-bit T2s and 32-bit T4s; and by hardware on the T8s. Notice the comparative speed for REAL32 arithmetic.

Table 5.4 Number of cycles for various operations.

	Time (in cycles; 1 cycle = 5 x 10^{-8} secs)		
Constant	1		
Variable name	2		
Assignment	1		
Error check	6		
Input, output Primitives	28		
SEQ	0		
IF	1		
n guards	4n		
ALT	31		
n guards	20n		
PAR n components	30n-11		
WHILE	12		
SEQ i = 0 FOR n	15n-4		
PAR i = 0 FOR n	71n-6		
REAL32 floating point	T2	T4	T8
+ -	705	300	7
*	705	240	13
/	1,410	280	19

5.7.1 Sequential program (PIPESEQ)

From Listings 3.2 and 3.3 we find that the following require approximately:

`SEQ r = 1 FOR R`	(15R-4) cycles
`SEQ n = 1 FOR N`	(15N-4)R cycles
`est := x*Half`	250R cycles
`est := (est + x/est) *Half`	840NR cycles
`x:= REAL32 ROUND R`	10R cycles

giving a total calculation time T_{calc} of about R[855N + 270] cycles.

The data given in Table 5.4 are approximate and INMOS obtained them from detailed simulation; in particular we have cited the worst case data for the floating point operations. Further, there are several varieties of each processor type (T414, T212) with different clock rates; we have adopted the rate of 50 ns for one cycle.

Thus, for R = 2 x 10^4 integers:

$$T_{calc} = 2 \times 10^4 \times 5 \times 10^{-8} [855N + 270] \text{ secs}$$

$$= (0.855N + 0.270) \text{ secs}$$

and the calculation time clearly varies linearly with N. For example, with N = 10, T_{calc} is 8.8 secs, compared with the value of 9.4 seconds from Table 5.2.

5.7.2 Parallel program (PIPEPAR)

A similar analysis for the code in Listings 3.6 and 3.7 gives T_{calc} = 0.91N +0.37 (compare this with the (0.85N + 0.27) for the SEQ program; the difference is mostly due to the `PAR n = 1 FOR N` replicator which takes 71NR cycles). With N = 5 and 10, this gives 4.9 secs and 9.5 secs which compare quite closely with 6.2 and 11.6 secs respectively, as given in Table 5.2. This illustrates the overhead associated with implementing `PAR`s on a single transputer.

However, for N = 20, T_{calc} is 18.6 secs compared with 31.1 secs from the table! Why this sudden discrepancy? The overhead of the PARs is not large enough to explain it. Table 5.5 contains the answer; it gives the size in bytes (using decimal numbers) of the compiled occam code, and the work space for scalar variables and for vectors (arrays).

On the transputers used here, the total on-chip memory space is 2k (2048) bytes – (4k on more recent ones); scalars are stored first, at the low addresses; then the vectors; and finally the compiled code. If there is not sufficient space on-chip, external memory is used, to which access is much slower. With N = 5 and 10, all the data is stored on-chip with some of the code in external memory; for N>10, increasingly more of the data is in the external memory; hence the reduction in performance as measured in MFlops as N increases beyond 10.

Table 5.5 Code and Variable Sizes (in bytes) for the PIPEPAR program.

N	**Code**	**Work Space**	**Vector**	
5	1,596	668	24	variables on chip
10	1,600	1,168	44	
20	1,604	2,168	84	increasingly more
40	1,604	4,168	164	variables in
80	1,604	8,168	324	external memory
		100N+168	4N+4	↓

For comparison Table 5.6 gives the code and variable storage for the "PIPESEQ" and "Hi there" programs, each of which is stored in on-chip memory. These storage values can be obtained by loading the appropriate program, using @F2 and then entering the appropriate code fold.

Table 5.6 Code and variable sizes (in bytes) for PIPESEQ and 'Hi There' programs

Program	**Code**	**Work Space**	**Vector**
PIPESEQ			
(all N)	1,424	112	0
Hithere	688	68	0

5.7.3 The network program (PARREAD)

Communication time

For processing R integers through the pipeline of M transputers (with the assumption M << R) then the total communication time T_{comm} is approximately R times the time for one communication (ignoring the small effect of priming and flushing the pipeline). For each of the R integers, the data communicated is two 32-bit reals (`x, est`) occupying 8 bytes.

$T_{comm} \cong 8 / 400 \times 10^3 R = 2 \times 10^{-5} R$ secs

assuming a link communication speed of 400 kbytes/sec (INMOS data).

Calculation time

The pipeline operates at the speed of its slowest member, so that from Listing 5.2 again using the data in Table 5.4, we find:

$$T_{calc} \cong 2{,}850 \text{ R Nits cycles}$$

$$= 1.4 \times 10^{-4}\ R\lceil N/M \rceil \text{ secs}$$

where $\lceil . \rceil$ indicates the least integer greater than.

For R = 20000, this is $T_{calc} = 2.85 \lceil N/M \rceil$ secs, with $T_{comm} = 0.4$ secs, which over-estimates the figures found in Table 5.3 (again, worst case data for floating point times were given in Table 5.4). The configuration information similar to Figure 5.2 shows that all code and data is in on-chip memory.

Load balance

The total computation time T_M is

$$T_M = T_{comm} + T_{calc}$$

$$= 2 \times 10^{-5} R + 1.4 \times 10^{-4} \lceil N/M \rceil R$$

$$= 10^{-5} R\ [2 + 14\lceil N/M \rceil]$$

so the efficiency is $(2 + 14N)100 / M\ [2 + 14\lceil N/M \rceil]$

From these we can understand the behaviour in Table 5.3. First, as the number, M, of transputers is increased, the first term in T_M is constant, but the second decreases; that is, the ratio of communication:calculation increases, and the efficiency decreases. Secondly, as N increases, the amount of work per transputer increases and the communication:calculation ratio decreases and the efficiency improves. We can generalise this in the following way: for a pipeline of M transputers, each of which does the same amount of calculation we can write:

$$T_M = T_{comm} + T_{calc}$$

$$= C_{comm} R + C_{calc} R/M$$

where C_{comm}, C_{calc} are coefficients determining the amount of communication and calculation, respectively. Let $\alpha = C_{comm}/C_{calc}$. Then:

$$E_M = (C_{comm} + C_{calc}) / M(C_{comm} + C_{calc} / M)$$

$$= (\alpha + 1) / (M\alpha + 1)$$

Now, as α --> 0, E_M --> 1; when communications are low, the efficiency is high because each transputer is kept busy. As α --> ∞, E_M --> 1/M; when communications are high, the efficiency decreases with increase in the number of transputers because each cannot be supplied with sufficient work to keep it busy.

Returning to the Newton-Raphson scheme, we can use these formulas to investigate the effect of changing from the slow T2s to T4s and the fast T8s (See Table 5.4 for relative speeds). For the (slow) T2 network used above, $\alpha_2 = 1/(7N) < 1/7$, so the communications are relatively low. If we replace the T2s with T4s, we have $\alpha_4 = {}^1/_{(2N)}$ and the network is communication bound for small values of N. For T8s, $\alpha_8 = 10/N$, which is large for values of N up to ~30.

Conclusion

This Section has shown that it is possible to assess approximately the performance of a program on a network, using the data supplied by INMOS. The performance figures are degraded if the data and/or program are stored off-chip. Load balance and efficiency estimates depend strongly on the ratio of communication time to calculation time, the latter also depending on the speed of the processor. Whilst increasing the number of transputers in a network can reduce total processing time, they may be inefficiently used.

Exercises

1. Run the Newton-Raphson program for a network PARREAD.TOP, with `R` = 20000 for values of `N` = 5, 10, 20, 40, 80, and various numbers of transputers in the network (Eg. `M` = 1, 2, 3, ...), to obtain timings as in Table 5.3.

To change the number of transputers involves changing the value of `M` in the `VALs` fold in the `PROGRAM`. Then recompile and reconfigure, and change the wiring of the network.

2. Using the data in Table 5.4, obtain T_{calc} for PIPEPAR.TOP as in Section 5.7.2.

3. How could you modify PARREAD.TOP so that `M` could be read in, so avoiding repetition? (Hint, read in a maximum value for `M`.)

4. In Listing 5.2, in the `feed and bleed` and `finished and pause` folds, there are initial indentations of two spaces. This rather poor programming style arises because the variable `INT Any`, in fold `running`, was introduced to allow a pause for starting and stopping the stop watch, when running the program. It is preferable that first lines in folds are not indented in this way. How could the program be changed to avoid this?

6

The processor farm

6.1 Introduction

In this chapter we look at a second form of parallelism which is rapidly becoming a "standard" (Processor Farms); and also at servers, which allow programs to be run independently of the TDS. For example, you may wish to use the graphics of the host computer, or add some feature to the server not already provided by INMOS, such as handling interrupts from a frame grabber, or sending output to a second computer.

In the previous chapters we have investigated pipelines, where the algorithm was decomposed into a number of smaller sequential stages, all the stages operating in parallel. Speed-up occurred only if there were many sets of data to be processed, with the speed-up being approximately proportional to the number of processors used. The pipeline can, however, only operate at the speed of its slowest stage.

We now turn to a second form for the parallelism where the work can be decomposed into smaller, independent portions, with the amount of calculation normally varying from portion to portion. These are "farmed out" to the processors in the network by a controller process, which also receives returning results and sends them on for display. Each transputer in the network is also responsible for routing the incoming and outgoing data. Load balancing (the apportioning of the work whilst trying to keep each transputer busy) is automatic.

The application running on the farm is, in the present case, the ubiquitous Mandelbrot set generator, with the results displayed on the IBM PC graphics screen, via the BIOS (the Basic Input Output System). This entails creating a "stand-alone" program (that is, one that can run independently of the TDS) which contains low-level interrupt procedure calls (not available from the TDS) to access the graphics through the BIOS.

The afserver (Alien File Server) is used to run this from MS-DOS (see Section 6.4); a server is a program which boots a network and provides host support (such as IO).

Some further occam is introduced: the use of `CASE` with variant protocols, the passing of array segments along channels between processors of different types, the use of `PRI ALT` and `PRI PAR`, and the primitive type `TIMER`. We also illustrate the use of `af.multiplexor` (a procedure within the `afserver` library `afinterf`) which allows multiplexing of the `screen` and `keyboard` channels, if more than one process needs access to them.

6.2 The Mandelbrot program

To illustrate the use of a farm, we shall use the Mandelbrot set generator. The generator is an iterative, complex valued algorithm which associates a colour with each graphics-screen position (x,y); this colour is determined by whether or not the point lies in the Mandelbrot set. A complex number is considered in the set if the number of iterations reaches a given fixed number (typically 250 or 1000), whilst its modulus remains less than 2. If the point is in the set, its colour is black; otherwise the colour reflects the number of iterations reached when the modulus exceeds 2. Before the iterations are applied, we must transform from screen co-ordinates (x,y) to a standard square area of side 2c:

$$\bar{x} = c[2(x - x_0)/(x_m - x_0) - 1]$$
$$\bar{y} = c[2(y - y_0)/(y_m - y_0) - 1]$$

where (x_0, y_0) is the screen origin, (x_m, y_m) the opposite corner, and c is assumed to be 2.

The iterations are then:

$$z_0 = 0$$
$$z_{n+1} = z_n * z_n + (\bar{x} + i\bar{y})$$

and the Mandelbrot algorithm, written in pseudocode is:

```
FOR each screen pixel (x,y)
  It.No = 0
  Transform to (x̄,ȳ) co-ordinates
  z = 0
  WHILE (It.No < ManConst) AND (|z| < 2)
    z = z*z + (x̄ + iȳ)
    It.No = It.No + 1
                          BLACK, IF It.No = ManConst
Plot Colour (x,y) =
                          It.No REM No.Colours, otherwise
```

where `ManConst` is the fixed constant mentioned above; a larger constant implies more calculation for pixels within the set. The amount of computation also varies from pixel to pixel.

6.3 Farms

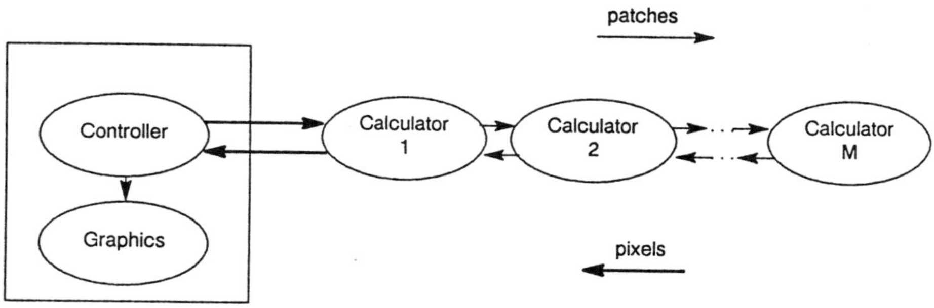

Figure 6.1 Processor farm

Figure 6.1 shows a controller handing out the work to the calculators, and receiving the processed pixels for sending on to display on the screen by the graphics process. Each of the M transputers in the network runs the same calculator process, but on different data. How should the work be divided amongst the processors? If, for example, the screen were divided into M equal areas and an area sent to each transputer, the load would be very uneven, since the amount of computation varies from pixel to pixel. Some transputers would stand idle, whilst the others completed their tasks. A better method, which achieves automatic load balancing, is for the controller to hand out one point to each calculator. When this has computed the colour of the pixel and returned it for display, the controller sends another point to this calculator. However this is likely to be wasteful of the calculating power of the transputer so instead of sending just one point at a time, the screen is split into patches of points (a fraction of a screen row in our case), with the idea of increasing the ratio of computation to communication (but see Section 6.7). The Controller works sequentially through the screen row by row, sending the start, end and row number of each patch to the network. When it finishes, it sends a termination signal.

Each transputer also routes data: the outgoing patches of work; and the incoming packets of pixels.

6.3.1 The calculator

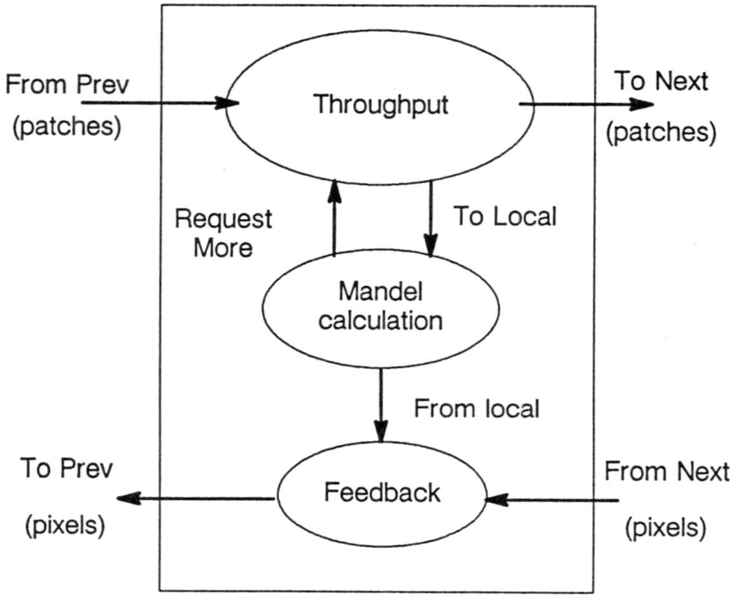

Figure 6.2 Processes running on each calculating transputer

The calculator contains three processes: `Throughput`, `Mandel.calc` and `Feedback`.

(i) `Throughput` receives patches from these previous transputer. If the local calculator is busy, it passes the patch to the next processor, otherwise it gives it to the local calculator.

(ii) `Mandel.calc` carries out the Mandelbrot calculation for the patch of points, and passes the pixels to `Feedback` as soon as it is finished. It then sends a request to `Throughput` for another patch.

(iii) `Feedback` multiplexes the pixels from the local Mandel calculator, and from the next transputer along in the farm.

The message passing between transputers is given a higher priority than the calculation (see Section 6.5.7) – otherwise another transputer in the system could be held up waiting for something to do.

These processes are terminated when each has finished its job. When `Throughput` receives a close down signal from the previous transputer, it waits until it receives its next (final) request from its local Mandel calculator, and then passes the terminate signal on to the next transputer, and also to the local calculator, and then closes down. When `Mandel.calc` receives a terminate signal, it sends it on to `Feedback` and closes down. `Feedback` cannot close down until both its local processor has finished and also the next transputer up the farm. When this occurs, `Feedback` sends a halt signal to the previous transputer and terminates itself.

6.3.2 The last transputer in the farm

Clearly, the last transputer cannot send on patches, nor receive pixels from the next one up the line. In the program, a check is made to detect the last transputer and deal with it specially.

6.3.3 Avoiding a log-jam

If all the processors are busy calculating, why doesn't the system clog up as the controller continues to send out patches? The answer lies in the rendezvous; when all the processors are busy, the rendezvous between the `controller` and the first transputer in the network cannot be completed until the `Throughput` process is free to receive another patch. Until this occurs, the `send patches` part of the controller suspends operation temporarily. Eventually, one of the calculators will finish and the log jam will be removed.

An alternative to this is to incorporate a valve mechanism in the controller, which counts out patches and counts back pixel packets; when the difference between these reaches the number of transputers in the network, the valve shuts down the `send patches` until a transputer becomes free, i.e. when the count back increases by one.

6.4 The graphics

The TDS does not have any facilities for accessing the IBM PC graphics screen (`screen` and `keyboard` channels do not encompass this); however, we can use interrupts through the BIOS. This requires running a "stand-alone" program: we first develop a program using the usual TDS facilities, and, when it is working correctly, turn it into one which can be run by the `afserver` (it is called MANNET.B4 in the present case). A server is a program which boots a network and provides host support, such as IO facilities.

To run such a stand-alone program, type (from MS-DOS):

```
afserver -:b mannet.b4
```

The pixels are plotted one by one. The calculators send back to the controller a data packet consisting of the start and end of the patch, its row number and an array segment containing the colours of each pixel.

6.5 Explanation of the program

Listings 6.1 to 6.11 show the program for the Mandelbrot processor farm (MANNET). It is rather lengthy and is best understood when using the folding editor in the TDS. In removing the folds to list the programs on paper, some of the hierarchical clarity is inevitably lost. To aid with the reading, we have inserted occasional ----- lines; these, of course, do not form part of the program. Further, SC units and most procedures are listed in separate Listings.

```
{{{F MANNET.TOP
... PROGRAM mannet
}}}

{{{ PROGRAM mannet
...F mannet
...F code
...F descriptor
...F CODE PROGRAM mannet
}}}

{{{F mannet
... PROTOCOLs16
... SC Controlprog
... SC Mandel
... Configuration
}}}
```

Listing 6.1 Top level folds for Mandelbrot farm (MANNET)

Listing 6.1 shows the top level folds. Note, since we are using the afserver, there is no EXE fold, just one PROGRAM fold. There are two SCs at this level: Controlprog run on the B004 host transputer and Mandel run on each of the processors in the farm.

6.5.1 PROTOCOLs

The protocols (Listing 6.1) must be defined at this point as they are required in the SCs Controlprog and Mandel, and also in the Configuration fold. In fact, as usual, they are defined again at the start of each of these SC folds (see Listings 6.4 and 6.8); however, it is incorrect to move the definition to follow these SCs, to precede Configuration – this causes the TDS to jam at compile time.

```
{{{ PROTOCOLs16
... Coordinates
... Pixels
}}}

{{{ Coordinates
PROTOCOL Coordinates
  CASE
    Coords; INT16; INT16; INT16
    Mandel; INT16; INT16; INT16; INT16
    terminate
:
}}}

{{{ Pixels
PROTOCOL Pixels
  CASE
    Pixel ; INT16; INT16; INT16; INT16::[]INT16
    halt
:
}}}
```

Listing 6.2 The PROTOCOLS (MANNET)

There are two sets of protocol defined:

❑ `Coordinates` for sending data to the network; and

❑ `Pixels` for receiving data from the farm.

Notice that each set is preceded by the word `PROTOCOL`, and ended with a "`:`".

Since differently structured data can be sent down the same channel, we have to cater for all variations of structure. Coordinates has three protocols, tagged with `Coords`, `Mandel` and `terminate`. `Coords` allows for sending a packet of three `INT16`s (`patch.start, patch.end and row` – see Listing 6.6 for an example); `Mandel` defines a packet of four `INT16`s, used for sending the Mandelbrot constant, the screen size and the maximum number of colours available for plotting, to each of the calculators in the network initially (see Listing 6.6); and `terminate` which is a tag used to indicate that all the patches have been sent. The tag proceeds the data down the channels; in the last case, only the tag is sent, no data being needed.

The `Pixels` `PROTOCOL` is used for returning packets of pixels, or a close down tag `halt`, when all processing is complete on a particular processor. The pixel packet consists of the start and end pixel, the row number and the colours of the pixels in the packet (see, for example, Listing 6.6, `received pixels` fold). The protocol structure is three INT16s followed by a "counted array"; in this case an INT16 indicating the size of the INT16 array segment to follow, the :: separator and the type of segment itself, []INT16. Array segments (or slices, as they are also known) are an efficient way of sending blocks of data down a channel; the range of subscripts is enclosed in square brackets [], using FROM and FOR:

```
size :: [arrayname FROM start FOR count]
```

where, normally, size and count are the same variable (but see Section 6.5.5, for further details). By this means only the "active" part, as determined by No.Pixels (which in turn depends on the number of patches / row), of the array Col.Its is communicated.

In declaring the PROTOCOLs, note the use of CASE when there are several tags and the indentation required by the syntax: 2 columns following PROTOCOL, 2 following CASE.

The reason INT16 is used everywhere is again because of the T2 in the network farm. The consequences of this are discussed later (Section 6.5.5). If T4s were used in the network, this system would still work, though INT16 would not be strictly necessary; INT could be used in its place.

6.5.2 Configuration

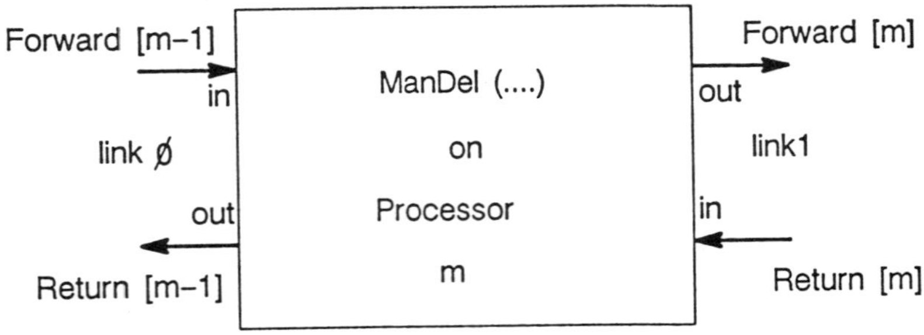

Figure 6.3 Link placements on mth transputer

```
{{{ Configuration
... VALS
... HARD CHAN data
... CHANs

PLACED PAR
  PROCESSOR 0 T4
    PLACE Forward[0] AT link2out:
    PLACE Return[0] AT link2in:
    PLACE From.Server AT link0in :
    PLACE To.Server AT link0out :
    Controlprog(From.Server, To.Server, Forward[0],
                Return[0])

  PLACED PAR m = 1 FOR M
    PROCESSOR m T2
      PLACE Forward[m-1] AT link0in:
      PLACE Forward[m] AT link1out:
      PLACE Return [m-1] AT link0out:
      PLACE Return [m] AT link1in:
      ManDel( Forward[m-1], Forward[m], Return[m-1],
              Return[m],m, M)
}}}

{{{ VALS
VAL M IS 3:
}}}

{{{ HARD CHAN data
VAL link0out IS 0:
VAL link1out IS 1:
VAL link2out IS 2:
VAL link3out IS 3:
VAL link0in  IS 4:
VAL link1in  IS 5:
VAL link2in  IS 6:
VAL link3in  IS 7:
}}}

{{{ CHANs
[M+1] CHAN OF Coordinates Forward:
[M+1] CHAN OF Pixels Return:
CHAN OF ANY From.Server, To.Server:
}}}
```

Listing 6.3 The configuration fold (MANNET)

Figure 6.3 shows the link placements for each of the transputers, and Listing 6.3 the corresponding code. Hard channels of `Coordinates` and `Pixels` are declared, the number of them depending on the number M of transputers in the farm.

The `CHAN OF ANY From.Server, To.Server` allows the T4 to communicate with the afserver, via the `af.multiplexor` (see Section 6.5.3). The `ANY` indicates the channel will accept any type of data format, and is an anachronism to maintain compatibility with earlier versions of the TDS. We placed `Controlprog` on the T4, Processor 0; and a copy of `ManDel` on each of the T2s in the farm, the first of which is Processor 1 (we already used "0" for the T4, and can not use it again).

6.5.3 The Controlprog SC (on the B004)

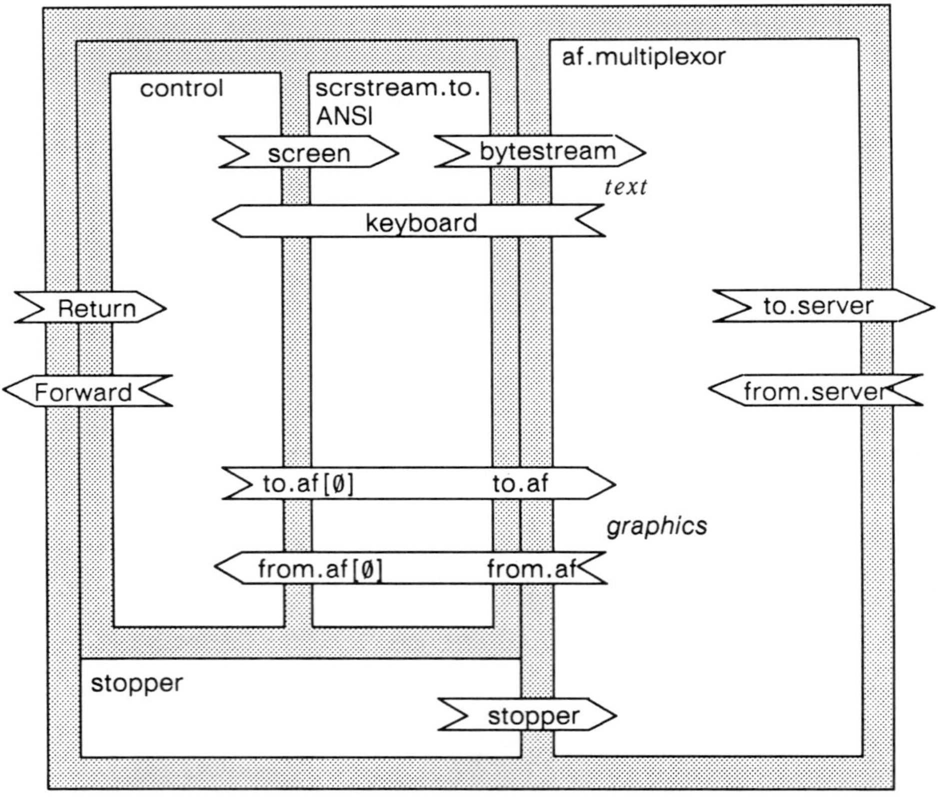

Figure 6.4 The Controlprog SC: processes and channels

Figure 6.4 shows the processes and channels of the `SC Controlprog`; and Listing 6.4 the corresponding occam code.

Start of Listing 6.4:

```
{{{ SC Controlprog
...F Controlprog
...F code
...F descriptor
...F link
...F debug
...F CODE SC Controlprog
}}}

{{{ Controlprog
#USE interf
#USE afinterf
#USE afiler
... PROTOCOLs16
... PROC ControlProg
}}}

{{{ PROC ControlProg
PROC Controlprog(CHAN OF ANY from.server, to.server,
                 CHAN OF Coordinates Forward,
                 CHAN OF Pixels Return)
  ... CHANs for af
  ... VALs for af

  ... PROC Control

  PAR
    ... Call Control PROC
    ... af multiplexor
:
}}}
------------------------------------------------------------
{{{ CHANs for af
CHAN OF INT keyboard:
CHAN OF ANY screen:
CHAN OF BYTE bytestream:
CHAN OF BOOL stopper:
CHAN OF BYTE error.not.used:
[1] CHAN OF ANY to.af, from.af:
}}}

{{{ VALs for af
VAL one.hundredth.of.a.sec IS 150:
}}}
```

```
{{{ Call Control PROC
SEQ
  PAR
    scrstream.to.ANSI (screen, bytestream)
    Control (keyboard, screen, to.af[0], from.af[0],
               Forward, Return)
  stopper ! TRUE
}}}

{{{ af multiplexor
af.multiplexor (bytestream, keyboard, error.not.used,
                to.af, from.af,
                from.server, to.server, stopper,
                one.hundredth.of.a.sec)
}}}
```

Listing 6.4 The Controlprog SC (MANNET)

At the outer level, the program's main function is to receive the pixels from the farm and to send them on to the graphics screen along the channel `to.server`, capable of accepting afserver command protocol (see `call.interrupt` in Section 6.5.6). In fact, this interrupt procedure also requires acknowledgment from the server, so a `from.server` channel is needed, too. Since the program runs independently of the TDS, using the afserver, we make use of the combination of the process `af.multiplexor` (found in the library `afinterf`) and `scrstream.to.ANSI` (in `interf`). The latter process, running in parallel with the `Control` procedure, converts the TDS screen protocol used in some of the processes within `Control` into a stream of bytes (`bytestream` channel) which will drive the terminal of the IBM host computer. For example (as shown in Listing 6.5) `write.full.string` and `read.echo.int` are TDS screen protocol; as we developed the program on the host under the TDS, we naturally used this protocol. When the time came to convert the program to a stand-alone one, rather than have to convert all such protocols to another, using the editor, the `afserver` system provides the `scrstream.to.ANSI` which accomplishes this end.

Because the server needs to handle the channels `bytestream`, `keyboard` and `to.af`, `from.af` (for the graphics) we use the `af.multiplexor` to communicate with the host file server. `stopper` is a channel to close down the multiplexor and return to MS-DOS when all processing is complete. The other two parameters of `af.multiplexor` are `error.not.used` and `one.hundredth.of.a.sec`; the former, as the name suggests, is not used; the latter indicates the frequency of polling for keyboard input. `afiler` is a library containing file handling procedures, used in communicating along the channels to and from the host.

It is also important that we terminate the `scrstream` process correctly, by sending it a terminate character along the `screen` channel; this can only be done at the end of the `Control` procedure described in the next Section. Note the anachronistic use of `CHAN OF INT` with `keyboard`, and `CHAN OF ANY` with `screen`.

6.5.4 The procedure Control

This is essentially the processes illustrated in Figure 6.1: the controller and the graphics handler (each of which is written as an `SC`) with the addition of some start up and close down processes, and the timing device.

Start of Listing 6.5:

```
{{{ PROC Control
PROC Control (CHAN OF INT keyboard,
              CHAN OF ANY screen, to.filer, from.filer,
              CHAN OF Coordinates ToMandels,
              CHAN OF Pixels FromMandels)

  ... Control prog body
:
}}}

{{{ Control prog body
#USE userio
#USE interf

... SC PROC Controller
... SC PROC Graphics

... CHANs
... vars for graphics
... VALs

SEQ
  ... started running message
  ... Input Number of Rows, cols, patches and Mandel Const
  ... timer set up

    PAR
      Graphics (ToGraphics, from.filer, to.filer)
      Controller (ToMandels, FromMandels, ToGraphics,
                  Sc.rows, Sc.cols, No.patches, ManConst,
                  max.x, max.y, max.colour)

    ... timer end
  ... print finished
  ... close down scrstream
}}}
```

Listing 6.5: page two

```
-------------------------------------------------------------
{{{ CHANs
CHAN OF Pixels ToGraphics:
}}}

{{{ vars for graphics
INT Sc.rows, Sc.cols, No.patches, ManConst:
}}}

{{{ VALs
VAL max.x IS 639:
VAL max.y IS 349:
VAL max.colour IS 15:
}}}

{{{ started running message
write.full.string (screen, "Started running --")
newline (screen)
INT Any:
keyboard ? Any
}}}
-------------------------------------------------------------
{{{ Input Number of Rows, cols, patches and Mandel Const
INT error:
SEQ
  ... Read rows
  ... Read cols
  ... Read patches
  ... Read ManConst
}}}

{{{ Read rows
error := 0
write.full.string (screen, "Type number of rows")
read.echo.int (keyboard, screen, Sc.rows, error)
newline (screen)
}}}

{{{ Read cols
error := 0
write.full.string (screen, "Type number of cols")
read.echo.int (keyboard, screen, Sc.cols, error)
newline (screen)
}}}
```

Listing 6.5: page three

```
{{{ Read patches
error := 0
write.full.string (screen, "Type number of patches")
read.echo.int (keyboard, screen, No.patches, error)
newline (screen)
}}}

{{{ Read ManConst
error := 0
write.full.string (screen, "Type ManConst")
read.echo.int (keyboard, screen, ManConst, error)
newline (screen)
}}}
----------------------------------------------------------
{{{ timer set up
TIMER clock:
VAL Ticks.Per.Sec IS 15625:
INT Start.tick, End.tick:
REAL32 Elapsed:
SEQ
  clock ? Start.tick
}}}

{{{ timer end
SEQ
  clock ? End.tick

  Elapsed := (REAL32 ROUND (End.tick MINUS Start.tick)) /
             (REAL32 ROUND Ticks.Per.Sec)

  ... Write time
}}}

{{{ Write time
newline(screen)
newline(screen)
write.full.string (screen, " Elapsed time is ")
write.real32(screen, Elapsed, 10, 2)
write.full.string(screen, " secs.")
newline(screen)
}}}
```

```
{{{ print finished
write.full.string (screen, "finished")
newline(screen)

INT Any:
keyboard ? Any
}}}

{{{ close down scrstream
write.endstream (screen)
}}}
```

Listing 6.5 The Procedure Control (MANNET)

The inputting of the data should be self-explanatory, but see Section 5.4.1 if you need a reminder. In `close down scrstream`, the `write.endstream (screen)` (found in the library `userio`) sends a termination signal to the `scrstream.to.ANSI` process, when all processing is completed.

We can arrange to time the running of the program by starting a "stop clock" when the controller first starts up and stopping it when the controller finishes. We define `clock` to be a channel of the primitive type `TIMER`; this is one that is always ready to output, and which can be read but not written to. The number of ticks per second is fixed by the hardware, and is 15625 on T4s and T2s. `MINUS` is subtraction using modulo arithmetic.

6.5.5 The procedure Controller

This is as described in Section 6.3.

Before starting up the farm proper, the controller broadcasts `ManConst,` maximum screen dimensions and colours to each of the processors.

Start of Listing 6.6:

```
{{{ SC PROC Controller
...F PROC Controller
...F code
...F descriptor
...F debug
}}}
```

Listing 6.6: page two

```
{{{ PROC Controller
#USE userio

... PROTOCOLs16
PROC Controller (CHAN OF Coordinates ToMandels,
                 CHAN OF Pixels FromMandels, ToGraphics,
                 VAL INT Sc.rows, Sc.cols, No.patches,
                 ManConst, max.x, max.y, max.colour)

  ... comment
  ... VARs

  SEQ
    ToMandels ! Mandel; INT16 (ManConst); INT16(max.x);
                 INT16(max.y); INT16(max.colour)
    patch.length := Sc.cols/No.patches

    PAR
      ... receive pixels
      ... send patches
:
}}}
-----------------------------------------------------
{{{ comment
-- sends patches of screen to be processed by Mandel.pixels
-- and receives back pixels which it forwards to the graphics
-- for display.
}}}

{{{ VARs
INT patch.length:
}}}
-----------------------------------------------------
{{{ receive pixels
INT16 patch.start, patch.end, row:
INT16 No.Pixels:
[255] INT16 Col.Its:
BOOL running:
```

```
SEQ
  running := TRUE
  WHILE running
    FromMandels ? CASE
      ... Received pixels; send to graphics
      ... stop running

  ToGraphics ! halt
}}}

{{{ Received pixels; send to graphics
Pixel; patch.start; patch.end; row;
         No.Pixels::[Col.Its FROM 0 FOR (INT No.Pixels)]
  ToGraphics ! Pixel; patch.start; patch.end; row;
         No.Pixels::[Col.Its FROM 0 FOR INT(No.Pixels)]
}}}

{{{ stop running
halt
  running := FALSE
}}}
------------------------------------------------------------
{{{ send patches
SEQ
  SEQ row = 0 FOR Sc.rows
    SEQ patch = 1 FOR No.patches
      ... send coords for this patch on this row

  ToMandels ! terminate
}}}

{{{ send coords for this patch on this row
INT patch.start, patch.end:
SEQ
  patch.start := (( (patch - 1) * patch.length) + 1)
  patch.end := (patch.start + patch.length) - 1
  ToMandels ! Coords; INT16(patch.start);
                      INT16(patch.end); INT16(row)
}}}
```

Listing 6.6 The Procedure Controller (MANNET)

We need to explain the `Received pixels; send to graphics` fold in some detail. We developed the program on the T4 alone and then converted it to run on the network; this proved to be non-trivial. On the T4 alone, correct code for sending back pixels from one Mandel process to the previous is:

```
ToPrev ! Pixel; patch.start; patch.end; row;
         No.Pixels::[Col.Its FROM 0 FOR No.Pixels]
```

with Pixel PROTOCOL:

```
INT:INT:INT:INT::[]INT
```

with a similar structure for the receiving process. When placed on a T2 network, this code fails, the problem arising from a conflict of the number of bits of (i) the count of the replicator; (ii) the integers on T4s and T2s; and (iii) the integers used in the `PROTOCOL`s on the channels connecting the T4s and T2s.

When the receiving process is placed on the host T4, with the sender on the T2, then the `INT`s of the `PROTOCOL`s would imply 32-bits at the receiving end, and 16 at the other, a situation leading to deadlock. Thus all the `INT`s must be changed to either `INT16` or `INT32`; let us assume, for definiteness, `INT16`. This, in turn, means the sending `size (No.Pixels)` must be redefined as `INT16`, which will then be in conflict with the type of the `count` of the array segment. The `count` of replicators must be, by default, of type `INT` – it is impossible to redefine this as `INT16` or `INT32`. Thus, the easiest solution is to redefine the `Pixel PROTOCOL` as `INT16` everywhere; and to define `No.Pixels` as a variable of type `INT16`, converting this by `INT(No.Pixels)` where needed for the `count` – see, for example, the `More pixels` fold in Listing 6.11. The moral of all this is to keep in mind the eventual network while developing a program; this will avoid much re-jigging of code later.

6.5.6 The procedure Graphics

The graphics process receives pixels from the controller and sends them on for display on the graphic screen via interrupts to the BIOS.

Start of Listing 6.7:

```
{{{ SC PROC Graphics
...F PROC Graphics
...F code
...F descriptor
...F link
...F debug
}}}
```

Listing 6.7: page two

```
{{{ PROC Graphics
#USE afiler
#USE userio
... PROTOCOLs16
PROC Graphics (CHAN OF Pixels FromControl,
                CHAN OF ANY from.filer, to.filer)

  ... comments
  ... Vars
  ... graphics PROCs

  SEQ
    ... set colour mode
    running := TRUE

    WHILE running
      FromControl ? CASE
        ... Pixels received; plot them
        ... stop running
:
}}}
------------------------------------------------------
{{{ comments
-- receives patch of pixels from controller and displays
-- them on the screen
}}}

{{{ Vars
INT16 patch.start, patch.end, patch.row:
INT16 No.Pixels:
INT col, row:
[255] INT16 Col.Its:
BOOL running:
INT colour:
}}}
------------------------------------------------------
{{{ graphics PROCs
... Set 16 colour mode
... Plot Pixel
}}}
```

Listing 6.7: page three

```
{{{ Set 16 colour mode
PROC Set16.Col.Mode()

  -- sets colour mode to 16 on IBM (640 x 350) pixels
  VAL registers IS [#10, #0, #0, #0, #0, #0, #0, #0, #0, #0] :
  VAL max.size IS 512:
  [max.size]BYTE record :
  INT result, size, flag :
  SEQ
    VAL []BYTE regs RETYPES registers :
    call.interrupt(from.filer, to.filer, 16, regs, flag,
                   size, record, result)
:
}}}

{{{ Plot Pixel
PROC PlotPixel(VAL INT col, row, VAL INT16 Colour)

  -- plots the pixel at (col, row) with colour Colour

  ... VALs
  ... Vars

  call.interrupt(from.filer, to.filer, 16, regs, flag,
                 size, record, result)
:
}}}

{{{ VALs
VAL AX IS (3072 + (INT(Colour))):
VAL registers IS [AX, 0, col, row, 0, 0, 0, 0, 0, 0] :
VAL max.size IS 512:
VAL []BYTE regs RETYPES registers :
}}}

{{{ Vars
[max.size]BYTE record :
INT result, size, flag :
}}}
-------------------------------------------------------
{{{ set colour mode
Set16.Col.Mode()
}}}
```

```
------------------------------------------------------------
{{{ Pixels received; plot them
Pixel; patch.start; patch.end; patch.row;
  No.Pixels::[Col.Its FROM 0 FOR (INT No.Pixels)]
  ... plot patch
}}}

{{{ plot patch
SEQ x = 0 FOR(INT No.Pixels)
  SEQ
    col := INT( (x + ( (INT(patch.start)) - 1) ) )
    PlotPixel(col, (INT(patch.row)), Col.Its[x])
}}}
------------------------------------------------------------
{{{ stop running
halt
  running := FALSE
}}}
```

Listing 6.7 The Procedure Graphics (MANNET)

Two procedures are defined `Set16.Col.Mode` and `PlotPixel`, each of which uses `call.interrupt` from the library `afiler`. This invokes an interrupt call on the IBM host, setting up values in its registers; on return from the interrupt, it receives back the (changed) values of the registers. On the IBM there are 10 2-byte registers (ie. 16 bits/register) ; in contrast, the occam program assumes 32-bit registers, and so a conversion is performed. Thus, for example, a value of hexadecimal 10 in the first register of the IBM switches on the 16 colour mode, when it receives the interrupt number 16 (the third parameter of `call.interrupt;` this signifies video IO). The parameters "flag, size, record and result" are not used here (they are the values returned by the interrupt from the IBM). The line:

```
VAL [] BYTE regs RETYPES registers:
```

retypes `registers` (320 bits) as an array `regs` of type `BYTE` (that is, an array of size 40), as required for the fourth parameter.

In `PlotPixel, registers` is set up to display the colour of the pixel at screen position (`row, col`); the 3072 is equivalent to 12 in AH (high byte) of the AX register, to plot a pixel, while the colour to plot goes in the low byte AL of AX.

Unfortunately, having done all this, there is, at present, a bug in the INMOS software which results in blocks of pixels being plotted incorrectly.

6.5.7 The procedure Mandel

Listing 6.8 corresponds to Figure 6.2. Note the `PRI PAR` to give priority to the communications. The transputer has just two queues for processes – high and low priority, respectively (see Section 6.8). Even if `PRI PAR` has more than two component processes only the first is given high priority, the rest being on the low priority queue. However, it is possible to give more than one process the same high priority, as here. The `PAR` following `PRI PAR` links `Throughput` and `Feedback` into one high priority process, `Mandel.calc` being of low priority.

```
{{{ SC mand
...F manprog
...F code
...F descriptor
...F link
...F debug
...F CODE SC mandel
}}}

{{{ manprog
... PROTOCOLs16
PROC ManDel( CHAN OF Coordinates FromPrev, ToNext,
             CHAN OF Pixels ToPrev, FromNext,
             VAL INT tran, No.Trans)

  ... PROC Throughput
  ... PROC Mandel.calc
  ... PROC Feedback

  ... CHANs

  PRI PAR
    PAR
      Throughput (FromPrev, ToNext, ToLocal, RequestMore)
      Feedback (FromLocal, FromNext, ToPrev)

    Mandel.calc (ToLocal, FromLocal, RequestMore)
:
}}}
------------------------------------------------------------
{{{ CHANs
CHAN OF Coordinates ToLocal:
CHAN OF Pixels FromLocal:
CHAN OF INT RequestMore:
}}}
```

Listing 6.8 The Procedure Mandel (MANNET)

6.5.8 The procedure Throughput

This is as described in Section 6.3.1. It receives

(i) co-ordinate patches from the previous transputer;

(ii) initialising data such as `ManConst`; and

(iii) a closing down signal.

Start of Listing 6.9:

```
{{{ PROC Throughput
PROC Throughput (CHAN OF Coordinates FromPrev, ToNext,
                 ToLocal, CHAN OF INT RequestMore)
  ... comment
  ... Vars

  SEQ
    Mandel.Busy := FALSE
    running := TRUE

    WHILE running
      PRI ALT
        ... request from Mandel
        ... input from previous
    ... send terminate to next if not last transputer
    ToLocal ! terminate
:
}}}
-------------------------------------------------------
{{{ comment
-- Receives Coords from previous transputer and either
-- passes them on to the next
-- or keeps them for local processing
}}}

{{{ Vars
INT16 patch.start, patch.end, y:
INT16 ManConst, max.x, max.y, max.colour:
INT Any:
BOOL running, Mandel.Busy:
}}}
-------------------------------------------------------
```

Listing 6.9: page two

```
{{{ request from Mandel
RequestMore ? Any
  SEQ
    Mandel.Busy := FALSE
}}}
------------------------------------------------------------
{{{ input from previous
FromPrev ? CASE
  ... Patch received
  ... Receive ManConst and pass on
  ... Terminate received
}}}
------------------------------------------------------------
------------------------------------------------------------
{{{ Patch received
Coords; patch.start; patch.end; y
  IF
    ... Mandel not busy, send to Mandel
    ... Mandel busy, send to Next Transputer
}}}

{{{ Mandel not busy, send to Mandel
Mandel.Busy = FALSE
  SEQ
    ToLocal ! Coords; patch.start; patch.end; y
    Mandel.Busy := TRUE
}}}

{{{ Mandel busy, send to Next Transputer
Mandel.Busy = TRUE
  IF
    ... not last transputer
    ... last transputer
}}}
{{{ not last transputer
tran <> No.Trans
  SEQ
    ToNext ! Coords; patch.start; patch.end; y
}}}
```

Listing 6.9: page three

```
{{{ last transputer
tran = No.Trans
  SEQ
    RequestMore ? Any
    ToLocal ! Coords; patch.start; patch.end; y
    Mandel.Busy := TRUE
}}}
----------------------------------------------------------
----------------------------------------------------------
{{{ Receive ManConst and pass on
Mandel; ManConst; max.x; max.y; max.colour
  SEQ
    ... Send ManConst to Next
    ToLocal ! Mandel; ManConst; max.x; max.y; max.colour
}}}

{{{ Send ManConst to Next
IF
  ... not last transputer
  ... last transputer
}}}

{{{ not last transputer
tran <> No.Trans
  ToNext ! Mandel; ManConst; max.x; max.y; max.colour
}}}

{{{ last transputer
tran = No.Trans
  SKIP
}}}
----------------------------------------------------------
----------------------------------------------------------
{{{ terminate received
terminate
  SEQ
    ... If mandel is busy, wait for its final request
    running := FALSE
}}}
```

```
{{{ If mandel is busy, wait for its final request
IF
  Mandel.Busy = TRUE
    RequestMore ? Any
  TRUE
    SKIP
}}}

-------------------------------------------------------
{{{ send terminate to next if not last transputer
IF
  tran <> No.Trans
    ToNext ! terminate
  tran = No.Trans
    SKIP
}}}
```

Listing 6.9 The Procedure Throughput (MANNET)

`Throughput` required considerable thought and care in its design. The "obvious" way to deal with passing on co-ordinate patches is:

```
WHILE running
  SEQ
    FromPrev ? patch.start; patch.end; y

    ALT
      ToNext  ! patch.start; patch.end; y -- incorrect
      ToLocal ! patch.start; patch.end; y -- occam
```

This ensures that whichever guard in the `ALT` is ready will send the data. Unfortunately this is not correct occam, because `ALT` can only select on input and not on output (see Section 4.3.4). A solution to this, which we adopt here, is to have the receiving Mandel process issue a request when ready for more data; and to combine the input request into an `ALT` together with patch input along the channel `FromPrev` (see `PROC Throughput` in Listing 6.9).

The flag `Mandel.Busy` indicates that the process `Mandel.calc` is busy, so patches should be sent on to the next transputer in the farm. If the local calculator is free, on sending it the patch, `Mandel.Busy` is set `TRUE` immediately (see the fold `Mandel not busy, send to Mandel`).

We have given higher priority (`PRI ALT`) to the `request from Mandel` so that a free local calculator is given data in preference to sending it on to the next processor.

The `PRI` with `ALT` is unlike `PRI PAR` in that the priority applies to all component processes; when there is more than one ready guard, the one that is textually first is chosen.

For the last transputer in the farm, the patch cannot be sent on and must be processed locally, as soon as the `Mandel.calc` process becomes free: the `RequestMore? Any` in the fold `Mandel busy, last transputer` waits until `Mandel.calc` sends a message along the channel `RequestMore` (see Listing 6.10).

6.5.9 The Procedure Mandel.calc

This is as described in Section 6.2 and is given in Listing 6.10. Note the conversion from `INT16` to `INT` in several places, for the reasons explained in Section 6.5.5.

In the fold `determine colour`, we have included some alternatives as comments (e. g. `--INT16 (tran * 2))` – their use will be explained in Section 6.6.

Start of Listing 6.10:

```
{{{ PROC Mandel.calc
PROC Mandel.calc (CHAN OF Coordinates ToLocal,
                  CHAN OF Pixels FromLocal,
                  CHAN OF INT RequestMore)

  -- Receives a packet of co-ordinates
  -- and finds the colour associated with each pixel,
  -- according to Mandelbrot set

  ... Vars
  ... VALs

  SEQ
    running := TRUE
    WHILE running
      SEQ
        ToLocal ? CASE
          ... ManConst received
          ... terminate received
          ... Coords received;

    FromLocal ! halt
:
}}}
```

Listing 6.10, page two:

```
----------------------------------------------------------
{{{ Vars
INT ManConst, max.x, max.y, max.colour:
INT16 ManConst16, max.x16, max.y16, max.colour16:
INT xstart, xend, y:
INT16 patch.start, patch.end, row:
REAL32 xbar, ybar:
REAL32 X, Y, XY, Xsq, Ysq:
INT Pixel.No, It.No:
INT16 No.Pixels:
[255] INT16 Col.Its:
BOOL running:
}}}

{{{ VALs
VAL Any     IS 1:
VAL Zero    IS 0:
VAL One     IS 1:
VAL Two     IS 2.0 (REAL32):
VAL Four    IS 4.0 (REAL32):
VAL Zero32 IS 0.0 (REAL32):

VAL x0      IS 0:                  -- screen origin
VAL y0      IS 0:
VAL c       IS 2.0 (REAL32):       -- size of Mandelbrot
                                   -- square
VAL Twoc    IS 2.0 (REAL32) * c:
}}}

{{{ ManConst received
Mandel; ManConst16; max.x16; max.y16; max.colour16
  SEQ
    ManConst     := INT(ManConst16)
    max.x, max.y := INT(max.x16), INT(max.y16)
    max.colour   := INT(max.colour16)
}}}

{{{ terminate received
terminate
  running := FALSE
}}}
```

Listing 6.10: page three

```
-----------------------------------------------------------
{{{ Coords received
Coords; patch.start; patch.end; row
  ... process coords
}}}

{{{ process coords
SEQ
  xstart, xend := INT(patch.start), INT(patch.end)
        y := INT(row)

  Pixel.No := Zero
  No.Pixels := INT16 ((xend - xstart) + 1)
  SEQ x = xstart FOR(INT No.Pixels)
    SEQ
      ... Initialise Z etc

      WHILE (It.No < ManConst ) AND ((Xsq + Ysq) < Four)
        SEQ
          Xsq, Ysq := X * X, Y * Y
          XY       := X * Y
          X        := ((Xsq - Ysq) + xbar)
          Y        := ((Two * XY) + ybar)
          It.No    := It.No + One

      ... Determine colour of pixel

  ... send pixels
}}}
-----------------------------------------------------------
-----------------------------------------------------------
{{{ Initialise Z etc
It.No := Zero
X, Y  := Zero32, Zero32
Xsq, Ysq := X * X, Y * Y
... xbar
... ybar
}}}

{{{ xbar
xbar := (Twoc * ((REAL32 ROUND x) - (REAL32 ROUND x0)) )
xbar := (xbar / ((REAL32 ROUND max.x) - (REAL32 ROUND x0)) )
xbar := (xbar - c)
}}}
```

```
{{{ ybar
ybar := (Twoc * ((REAL32 ROUND y) - (REAL32 ROUND y0)) )
ybar := (ybar / ((REAL32 ROUND max.y) - (REAL32 ROUND y0)) )
ybar := (ybar - c)
}}}
------------------------------------------------------------
------------------------------------------------------------
{{{ Determine colour of pixel
IF
  ... In set therefore Black
  ... Not in set
Pixel.No := Pixel.No + One
}}}

{{{ In set therefore Black
It.No = (INT(ManConst))
  Col.Its [Pixel.No] := INT16 (Zero)
                             -- (INT16(5 + (tran*2)))
}}}
{{{ Not in set
It.No < (INT(ManConst))
  Col.Its [Pixel.No] := INT16( (It.No REM max.colour)
                             -- (INT16(tran*2))
}}}
------------------------------------------------------------
------------------------------------------------------------
{{{ send pixels
SEQ
  patch.start, patch.end := INT16(xstart), INT16(xend)
  row := INT16(y)
  FromLocal ! Pixel; patch.start; patch.end; row;
              No.Pixels::[Col.Its FROM 0 FOR(INT No.Pixels)]
RequestMore ! Any -- tell Throughput Mandel is now free
                  -- to process more
}}}
```

Listing 6.10 The Procedure Mandel.calc (MANNET)

6.5.10 The procedure Feedback

This is described in Section 6.3.1 and the code is in Listing 6.11. The process can terminate only when its local `Mandel.calc` has finished and also the next transputer up the farm; only then does it send a close down signal to the previous (`ToPrev ! halt`). On receiving such a signal from the next transputer, `more.from.next` is set `FALSE`.

Similarly, on receiving a close down signal from the local `Mandel.calc`, `more.from.local` is set `FALSE`. For the last transputer in the farm, in the absence of a signal from the previous transputer, `more.from.next` is set `FALSE` when `more.from.local` becomes `FALSE`.

Start of Listing 6.11:

```
{{{ PROC Feedback
PROC Feedback (CHAN OF Pixels FromLocal, FromNext, ToPrev)

  ... comments
  ... Vars

  SEQ
    ... set flags

    WHILE running
      SEQ
        PRI ALT
          ... FromNext
          ... FromLocal

        ... stop running?

    ToPrev ! halt
:
}}}
----------------------------------------------------------
{{{ comments
-- Passes on to previous Transputer the pixels from
-- local Mandelbrot patch or from next one up the farm
}}}

{{{ Vars
BOOL running, more.from.next, more.from.local:
INT16 xstart, xend, y:
INT16 No.Pixels:
[255] INT16 Col.Its:
}}}
{{{ set flags
more.from.local := TRUE
more.from.next := TRUE
running := TRUE
}}}
----------------------------------------------------------
```

Listing 6.11: page two

```
{{{ FromNext
(tran <> No.Trans) & FromNext ? CASE
  ... More pixels
  ... No more pixels
}}}

{{{ More pixels
Pixel; xstart; xend; y;
       No.Pixels::[Col.Its FROM 0 FOR (INT No.Pixels)]
  ToPrev ! Pixel; xstart; xend; y;
           No.Pixels::[Col.Its FROM 0 FOR (INT No.Pixels)]

}}}

{{{ No more pixels
halt
  more.from.next := FALSE
}}}
----------------------------------------------------------
{{{ FromLocal
FromLocal ? CASE
  ... More pixels received
  ... no more patches
}}}

{{{ More pixels received
Pixel; xstart; xend; y;
       No.Pixels::[Col.Its FROM 0 FOR (INT No.Pixels)]
  ToPrev ! Pixel; xstart; xend; y;
           No.Pixels::[Col.Its FROM 0 FOR (INT No.Pixels)]
}}}
{{{ no more patches
halt
  more.from.local := FALSE
}}}
----------------------------------------------------------
{{{ stop running?
... IF last transputer
... IF no more pixels and no more patches
}}}
```

Listing 6.11: page three

```
{{{ IF last transputer
IF
  (tran = No.Trans) AND (more.from.local = FALSE)
    more.from.next := FALSE
  (tran = No.Trans) AND (more.from.local = TRUE)
    SKIP
  TRUE
    SKIP
}}}

{{{ IF no more pixels and no more patches
IF
  (more.from.next = FALSE) AND (more.from.local = FALSE)
    running := FALSE
  TRUE
    SKIP
}}}
```

Listing 6.11 The Procedure Feedback (MANNET)

Comments on the Mandelbrot program

The Mandelbrot program is a working program, albeit perhaps not the most efficient in terms of the way the code is written, nor in the implementation (see Section 6.7 for a discussion of this). For example, in Listing 6.10, in the fold `ManConst received`, the variables `ManConst`, `max.x` etc. would give more efficient code if declared as constants:

```
VAL ManConst IS INT (ManConst16)
```

particularly as they are used in loops.

In developing the program, as usual we used the host alone, writing first the `Mandel.calc` process (Listing 6.11, minus the communications part) and then, when that was working, adding processes such as `Throughput` and `Feedback` and testing them on the host before transferring to the network. We spent most of the debugging time in terminating these additional processes gracefully. We tested each process in turn, starting with controller – the others being (`COMMENT`ed) out and then added one at a time, until all of them were working. Of course, just enough code was added at each stage to allow some progress to be made, the bodies of the processes being blank. The invaluable INMOS debugger, described in Chapter 7, was not available at the time; this would have saved enormous effort.

Further problems arose, as mentioned in Section 6.5.5, in converting the program to run on the network. These occurred because, whilst developing the programs, we had not thought sufficiently about the eventual configuration; the moral is to keep this in mind from the start.

In the working program there are some 60 lines of occam which perform the Mandelbrot calculation and 185 devoted to the farm structure and communications, this excluding control and graphics! Of course, once the farm is developed, it can be used for any other suitable program with relatively few changes – the structure of the data packages communicated (such as patches and pixels) must be altered accordingly. Several groups of researchers have developed "harnesses" along these lines.

6.6 Running on the network

After the usual compiling, configuring and extracting, you must create a stand-alone file MANNET.B4 – see stage (iv) below – and then run that.

(i) Compiling

- ❑ get utilities
- ❑ enter the `PROGRAM` and `mannet` folds
- ❑ compile `SC Controlprog` for a T4
- ❑ compile `SC Mandel` for a T2

(ii) `SC` extraction and configuring

- ❑ return to ...`PROGRAM` fold and press @5
- ❑ Configuring follows a successful extraction automatically.
- ❑ "Warning: 2 input link(s) and 2 output link(s) not connected" can be safely ignored – this refers to the Host links to the IBM.

(iii) Network extraction

- ❑ @3 extracts the code and puts it in the fold ...`F CODE PROGRAM mannet` in the `PROGRAM` foldset.
- ❑ WARNING: be careful not to press @F3 in mistake – you will apparently lose all your work! Don't panic: @F3 is "pick line" and places the fold in a buffer. To recover it, use SF3.

(iv) Creating an MS-DOS stand-alone file

- ❑ enter `PROGRAM` fold
- ❑ place cursor on `CODE PROGRAM` fold
- ❑ get file handling utilities @F5
- ❑ write Host @0
- ❑ change Host filename to mannet.b4

(v) exit from TDS

(vi) running stand-alone

```
afserver -:b mannet.b4
```

Note, if you need to recompile/reconfigure at a later stage, use @5 instead of stage (i), on the `...PROGRAM` fold. This recalls details of compilation (T2 or T4 target etc.) automatically, and then extracts and configures (i.e. without having to do stage (ii)).

6.7 Performance of the farm

Table 6.1 shows timings, speed-ups and efficiencies for several experiments, using a value of 250 for ManConst and 4 patches/row. The full screen was not used, two representative areas being chosen (100 x 100 and 200 x 200). The first area is "easy", in that the Mandelbrot calculation stops after only a few iterations everywhere i.e. these points are not in the Mandelbrot set. In the second, many full 250 iterations are performed, as can be seen from the times when the program was run on the host alone.

Table 6.1 Time (in secs), speed-up, S_m, and efficiency, E_m, for the Mandelbrot farm. (ManConst = 250, 4 patches/row)

Graphics area size		*100 x 100*			*200 x 200*	
Host alone (T4)		*6.3*			*171.0*	
Number of T2s in network	*Time*	S_m	E_m	*Time*	S_m	E_m
1	11.7	X	X	355.0	X	X
2	5.8	2.03	101	183.0	1.94	97
3	4.3	2.72	91	132.0	2.69	90

Comparison of the networks with 1, 2 and 3 T2s shows the speed-up, Sm, obtained; this is defined as the ratio of the time taken to run the program on one transputer to that on M. Again, as explained in Section 5.6, the T4 is not included in such calculations, the speed-ups being compared to the network consisting of 1 T2. The value of 2.03 with two T2s could be explained by discounting the T4, though it may be a real effect; other workers have also reported such super-linear speed-ups. Note, again, that 2 T2s are slower than the one T4 and 3 T2s are faster.

We timed the experiments in the table with the graphics plotting switched off (by COMMENTing out the appropriate bits of the graphics process and recompiling the program), since the many interrupt calls to the BIOS are very slow compared to the rate at which the network processes pixels; this, otherwise, would give unrealistic figures. As an example of the slowness using the BIOS, on an IBM XT, plotting 640 x 350 pixels of the Mandelbrot set takes several hours; on a Zenith Z-286 one hour or about 0.016 sec per pixel. This should be compared with a simple Pascal program to fill the screen – about 25 secs using "PutPixel".

In fact, when developing the program, we were not certain whether this slowness was due to slow plotting, a slow network or even if all the transputers were functioning correctly. To check this, instead of plotting the Mandelbrot set, we colour-coded a transputer according to its number in the network. For example, if a pixel were not in the Mandelbrot set, instead of sending back the corresponding colour (see Listing 6.10, `Determine colour of pixel` fold), we arranged to send `INT16 (2*tran)`, so that, for instance, transputer one is red, two green and three blue. This quickly showed that processor one dealt with the first patch, processor two with the second and processor three with all the other patches on the screen!

The explanation of this is that, because the plotting is so slow, a log-jam of pixels waiting to be plotted builds up quickly. The priorities ensure that the third processor's patches are returned first, so it deals with all the rest of the work. Processors one and two can send theirs back only after the third finishes! The cure is to hasten the graphics plotting and this we achieved using a graphics package written in occam (GAFS, 1989).

This, since it does not use the afserver directly, involved some considerable rewrite of the programs, which we have not presented here. Using this adapted program, measurements show that plotting one pixel now takes about 0.00013 secs compared with 0.016 secs using the BIOS approach. The colour coding of the processors then showed that each was taking its share of the processing. We found difficulty in following this when the processing reached the area of pixels in the Mandelbrot set. A further improvement overcame this problem, by sending back a lighter colour for a processor which is dealing with a pixel in the set, and this serves to indicate the outline of the Mandelbrot Figure, as the cover illustration of this book shows. Of course, this picture cannot show the order in which the patches are returned, as the "live" graphics do.

As anticipated in Section 6.3, we tried varying the number N of pixels in a patch to obtain some speed-up, but we were surprised to find this ineffective. For example, an area 100 x 600 pixels, with N = 2 took 24.2 secs; with N increased to 200 the time decreased, but to only 20.3 secs. The explanation is found in the next Section.

Atkin (1987) and Packer (1987) have suggested several further techniques, in addition to prioritised communication and packaging the pixels, for enhancing performance, including buffering. For example, by adding a buffer on the channel `To Local`, `Mandel.calc` can hold a patch ready to process immediately it finishes its current patch, rather than wait for one to be sent up the farm from the controller.

Buffers can also decouple processing on neighbouring transputers allowing calculation to proceed when it might have jammed otherwise. For instance, adding buffers to `Feedback`, one for use with the channel `From Local` and the other with `From Next` (see Figure 6.2), avoids a communication bottle-neck, and a consequent suspension of processing. To see this, suppose (without buffers) the channel `ToPrev[m]` cannot send data to transputer (m-1) because of some blockage down the farm (i.e. to the left in Figure 6.2) – this may simply be due to a heavy processing load. Then, the `Mandel.calc` on processor `m` cannot send processed data to its `Feedback` until `ToPrev[m]` is freed, which in turn means processor `m` will become idle, and so on, up the farm. By introducing a buffer, `Mandel.calc` can pass processed pixels to it and then immediately start on the next data from the `Throughput` buffer.

Packer (1987) has suggested a speed-up by a factor of two is thus possible. Atkin reports a little more conservative improvement – less than 1%. To investigate such questions, we can perform an analysis along the lines of that of Section 5.7. This we do in Section 6.9, but first a few words on scheduling parallel processes are necessary.

6.8 Scheduling parallel processes

On a transputer there can be only one process executing at a time, the others being suspended (waiting for completion of IO on a channel) or executable (waiting for their turn on the processor). There are just two queues for processes, high priority and low priority. Processes are placed on the high level queue via the use of `PRI PAR` in occam programs, as seen above. There is a different scheduling algorithm, implemented in hardware, for each of these queues. When a high level process becomes executable (after waiting to communicate, say), it has priority over an executing low priority one, which it will pre-empt.

Typically, this takes about 20 processor cycles, until the low level process can reach a point in its code where it can suspend (i.e., be placed on the low level queue). The high priority process cannot be pre-empted and continues executing until it terminates, stops, waits for communication or delays. When this occurs, if the high priority queue is empty, then a low level process is started from the low priority queue. The low level scheduler is round-robin, suspending the process in favour of another off the low level queue, after some 15000 to 30000 cycles, unless it first stops, waits for communication or a high priority process interrupts it.

6.9 Estimation of communication and computation times

Table 6.2 shows the number of processor cycles needed for the communications on the various channels and for the computations of the processes. We have assumed for simplicity that all data and program are stored on-chip. As this is certainly not the case, the estimates are optimistic, but they serve to explain the points observed in the last Section.

Table 6.2 Times (in processor cycles) for communications and computations in the farm.

Communications on Channel:	***Time in Cycles***
FromPrev, ToNext	320
ToLocal	6
RequestMore	2
FromLocal	2(N + 4)
FromNext, ToPrev	100(N + 4) + 20
Computation of process:	
ThroughPut, Feedback	10
Mandel.calc	$10^4 N(A + B.\bar{T})$

N is the number of pixels in a patch; $\bar{T}$ *is the average number of iterations for each pixel in the patch; A and B are coefficients depending on processor type – see Table 6.3*

6.9.1 Communications

From Listing 6.9, we see that each patch inputted to `Throughput` on the `FromPrev` channel consists of three `INT16`s, or 6 bytes, which, again assuming 400 k bytes/sec transmission rate with a processor cycle time of 50 ns, takes 300 cycles. The overhead in setting up a link transfer (i.e. the time it takes to suspend the current process and initiate transmission along a link; in the present case, `Mandel.calc` will be pre-empted by `Throughput` due to the `PRI PAR` in Listing 6.8) is typically about 20 cycles.

Once the transfer is started, it proceeds independently of the processor, which can thus immediately resume calculation. So the total time for patch transmission along `FromPrev` (and along `ToNext,` also) is about 320 cycles, which is independent of N, the number of pixels in a patch. In a similar way we find the returning processed pixel packets along the channels `ToPrev` and `FromNext` take about 100(N + 4) + 20 cycles. Between `Throughput` and `Mandel.calc` communications along `RequestMore` and `ToLocal` are about 2 and 6 cycles respectively; these are internal (soft) channels and require internal memory transfer only.

6.9.2 Computation

Analysing Listing 6.10, using a method similar to the one described in Section 5.7.3, we find the number of cycles/patch for the Mandelbrot calculations is approximately 10^4 N[0.98 + 0.58 $\overline{T}$], where $\overline{T}$ is the average number of times/pixel the `WHILE` loop is executed, for a particular patch. In general, we can write this as:

10^4 N[A + B.$\overline{T}$]

where A and B are constants depending on transputer type (T2, T4 or T8) as given in Table 6.3.

Table 6.3 Values of coefficient A and B by transputer type

	T2	T4	T8
A	0.98	0.34	0.020
B	0.58	0.23	0.018

Execution of the code for routing data via `Throughput` or `Feedback` takes about 10 cycles, which is tiny compared to the Mandel calculations.

6.9.3 Load balancing

We can now understand the results of the experiments of the last Section which used a network of T2s; that is, why, when plotting via the BIOS, one transputer alone does almost all the work; why increasing N, the number of pixels in a patch, has only a small effect on performance; and, finally, why buffers have little impact. We return to the use of networks of T4s and T8s afterwards.

Plotting a pixel via the BIOS is very slow compared to the rate of processing of patches by the T2s. For example, from Table 6.1, for one transputer we find the processing time for one pixel in the 100 x 100 area ($\overline{T} \sim 1.2$ here) is 0.0012 secs which is much smaller than the 0.016 secs plotting time. Three transputers, with $\overline{T} = 250$, produce pixels at about the plotting rate. Thus, for most pixels, a single transputer is capable of supporting the plotting.

The explanation of the two other results is that the computation time is already very high for T2s relative to communication times; increasing N or introducing buffers does not significantly change this. Patch data can be delivered quickly enough to keep all transputers busy and processed pixels can be returned efficiently. As soon as a `Mandel.calc` on a particular processor is finished, it requests more data and `Throughput` will input more from the previous processor. If it, the previous processor, is busy with its `Mandel.calc` (as is most likely) the high priority `PRI PAR` of Listing 6.8 given to `Throughput` will pre-empt this low level process and pass on the requested data. All this will be done within, typically, about 360 cycles, since computation of the two `Throughputs` take 20 cycles (see Table 6.2), suspension of the low level process 20 cycles and the data communication 320; this is small compared to the Mandelbrot calculation of about $10^4 N (0.98 + 0.58 \overline{T})$ cycles.

Even with a farm of several processors, the delivery time from the first to the last is small. Similarly, each pixel patch routed back will be delayed for approximately 30 cycles at each processor: 20 waiting for the low level process to suspend and 10 for the `Feedback` process. In this case, once the data transmission is initiated along the link, the `Mandel.calc` processing is resumed and done concurrently with the transmission. Transmission takes about 100(N+4) cycles, which again is very small compared with the computation time and does not inhibit return of pixels.

Now, any decrease in total computation time due to the increase of N is found in the reduction of overheads of communication, which arise chiefly in the number of times the low priority Mandelbrot calculations are suspended to allow communications to commence. After they have started, the communications place data directly into the memory and, at the same time, the processor resumes execution of the Mandelbrot process, so the actual transfer of data does not contribute to execution time. We can make a rough estimate of the effect of changing N on total execution time by counting the total number of communications that take place on the hard channels `FromPrev, ToPrev, ToNext and FromNext,` for each of which the Mandelbrot calculations suspend. There will also be a contribution from the soft channels `RequestMore, ToLocal` and `FromLocal;` for these, processes are not suspended, but there is some overhead in the simulated "transfer" of data along these channels. Let P be the total number of patches to be processed, so that ~P/M patches will be handled on each of the M transputers in the network. Then, for the first transputer in the network, which bears most of the communication load, we find the approximate overheads as:

`FromPrev`

20 cycles for suspension + 10 cycles for execution of the `Throughput` process, for

each patch from the `Controller`, giving 30P cycles for all P patches.

`ToPrev`

Similarly 30P, for all P patches to the `Controller`.

`ToNext and FromNext`

Approximately (M – 1)P/M patches are sent along `ToNext` to the second processor in the farm, and the same number received back along `FromNext`, so the number of cycles for `ToNext` and `FromNext` total 60(M-1)P/M.

`RequestMore, ToLocal and FromLocal`

These are internal (soft) channels and (using the data in Table 6.2) require about (2 + 6 + 2(N + 4)) cycles per patch for execution of their respective processes, or (16 + 2N)P/M in all.

For all communications on this processor the grand total is approximately (120P + 2(N – 22)P/M) cycles compared with the total computation time of 10^4N [1 + 0.5 $\bar{T}$]P/M cycles on each processor. For an area 100 x 600, P = 6.10^4 /N and the communication time overheads simplify to o(10^7 /N) and the calculation time per processor to o(10^9 /M), so the communication is swamped by the calculation. The decrease in total time between N = 2 and N = 300 due to reduced communication overheads is approximately 0.25 secs. This is smaller than the measured time we found in Section 6.7, but recall that we have ignored the effect of the slower access to external memory in this Section.

The first processor, of course, has roughly M times the number of communications to handle as the last one, but even with large numbers of T2s (say M = 100) the processing time is so large that the interrupts of the first processor would not be significant.

We now turn to a brief discussion of a network using faster transputers, in particular the floating point T8s. From tables 6.2 and 6.3, we see the Mandelbrot calculation takes about 200(1+$\bar{T}$)N cycles, with the switching time for `Throughput` 360 cycles, as above. Now, the communication is still o(10^7 /N) while the calculation time reduces to o(10^7 /M) cycles per processor, so, depending on the relative values of N and M, the calculation can be smaller than the communication overhead. For example, with N = 1, $\bar{T}$ = 1, the Mandelbrot calculation takes only 400 cycles, or about the same time as the switching; with N = 1, $\bar{T}$ = 10, five transputers would keep the first processor in the farm permanently occupied with communications. Hence, with T8s there is now a need for the buffering as discussed in Section 6.7.

Exercises

1. Compile and configure the program MANNET.TOP for use with the `afserver` (use filename MANNET.B4 – see Section 6.6).

2. Run for an area 100 x 100 pixels, using N = 4 and ManConst = 250. Note the time taken. Do you think all transputers are working? Check by colour coding the transputers (change the program in the process `Mandel.calc`, where the colours are assigned).

3. Switch off the graphics and run again for 1,2,3,... transputers. Calculate the speed-up and efficiency, as in Table 6.1. Are all transputers working?

4. Run with, for example, three transputers, for an area 100 x 600 with suitable values of N in the range N=2,..., 200, recording and plotting the times taken. (See Section 6.9.3).

5. If you have suitable software, rewrite the program to run with a graphics package such as GAFS, instead of via the BIOS, and record the times again.

6. Modify the program by adding buffers as discussed in Section 6.7 to see what difference (if any) they make.

7

Debugging concurrent programs

Every programmer knows how difficult it is to debug a sequential program, even with the use of disciplined development methods and with the aid of software tools such as debuggers. The task for concurrent programs is much more awesome, deadlock being an insistent problem. The programs presented in the previous chapters were not produced without a great deal of effort in getting them to work correctly. It seems at times that there is an unwritten law stating that any concurrent program will always end in deadlock! Unlike sequential programs, concurrent programs have the additional difficulty of sending print messages to the screen from parallel processes, and of gracefully terminating processes when execution is complete. The latter should be easy if you have developed your programs rigorously, as you should, but while learning occam this tends to be a secondary consideration.

In this chapter, we cover three debugging aids: first, the traditional do-it-yourself method of inserting print statements at well chosen points in the program; second, the software debugging tool provided with the TDS; and, last, another TDS tool known as a worm, which allows the integrity and correctness of the physical network to be checked and tested. In the remainder of this Section we give a brief introduction to each of these in turn.

DIY debugging

With the earlier versions of the TDS (700C and before), there was no software debugger and the usual fall back of inserting debug print statements, as you would with a sequential language, presents problems in a concurrent program. Two processes cannot simultaneously output to the `screen` channel, since the lines:

```
PAR
  screen ! message1
  screen ! message2
```

is illegal occam. This would give an interlaced message of characters from `message1` and `message2` , otherwise. So INMOS have provided a procedure

```
PROC scrstream.multiplexor ([] CHAN OF ANY screen.in,
                                  CHAN OF ANY screen.out,
                                  CHAN OF INT stopper)
```

which allows any one of the array of `screen.in` channels to grab the `screen.out` channel until its message is completely displayed. Then `screen.out` is released for the use of another input channel.

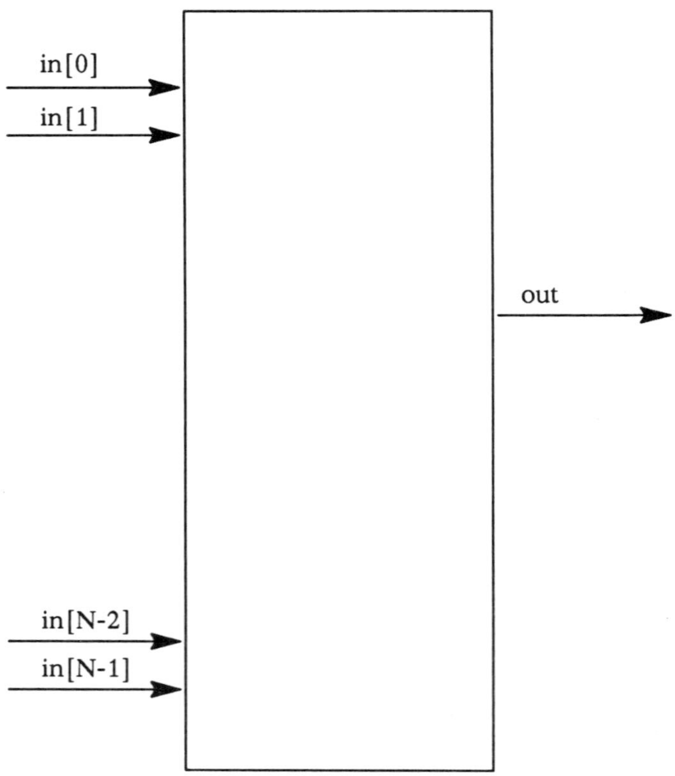

Figure 7.1 An N input Channel multiplexor

Figure 7.1 shows the structure of an N input channel multiplexor, for which the outline code is shown overleaf:

```
VAL N IS SIZE in:
SEQ
  running := TRUE
  WHILE running
    PRI ALT
     stop ? Any
       running := FALSE
     ALT n = 0 FOR N
       in[n] ? data
         out ! data
```

The `SIZE` in the `VAL` line assigns the number of elements in the input channel array `in[]` to `N`. The `PRI ALT` gives priority to the stop channel and the replicated `ALT` repeats the following process for the number of input channels. Once an input channel starts inputting it continues until all its data is transmitted to the `out` channel, and then another one is chosen at random according to the way the `ALT` is implemented in occam.

We shall use the `scrstream.multiplexor` by placing it in parallel with several concurrent processes which require debugging; Section 7.1. shows how this is done.

The debugger

Progress in developing a program is much enhanced with the use of the debugger. This is a software tool provided with the TDS, for post-mortem debugging of occam source code, running on a network of transputers. After invoking the debugger, you can inspect the processes which were running on each transputer, and display the values of associated variables and the contents of channels by moving the cursor around the screen to the appropriate point in the program. You can jump down channels from one process to another and investigate that. You can display the high and low priority queues of processes.

To use the debugger (see Section 7.2), an occam program must have been halted. For example you can interrupt a running or deadlocked program by using <CONTROL><BREAK>; or you can force a halt by writing a `STOP` process in the occam code; or the program might halt through execution errors, such as overflow or array bound violation.

Programs written as an `EXE`, or an `EXE + PROGRAM`, or a standalone program can be debugged. Once halted the TDS is rebooted, a core dump of all processes saved to a file, so that after the debugger is loaded and run on the offending occam program, it can be debugged.

The TDS 700D debugger has certain limitations; for example, you cannot set break points nor single step through programs.

The network tester

It is easy to make mistakes when wiring up a network; for example, if wrong connections are made then the loading will fail. Also, it is clearly important to ensure that the hardware functions properly, that the cables are indeed connected (this, we know, happens!) that they have good contacts, that links are set to correct speeds and so on. The network tester is a TDS tool which checks all is well in this area. It operates by sending out an exploratory program (a "worm") which finds its way from transputer to transputer, reporting back what it finds on the way. This includes the type of transputer (T2, T4, T8 etc.); the actual topology of the network; and the results of memory tests on each transputer. The network tester also checks the actual configurations with the one specified in your `PROGRAM`, reporting if the two match or how they differ, if they do not. It also indicates, for each transputer, which links are connected to which other processors, which links are not connected or gives an error message showing a problem on a particular link. The network tester is described in Section 7.3 .

The terms "analyse", "error" and "reset" occur frequently in the context of the debugger and network tester. Transputer networks must be analysed before the debugger can be used. Asserting analyse sends a signal from the host transputer to all transputers in a network telling them to halt at the next descheduling point, such as an input message or loop end. The state of the processors , for instance, values of variables, contents of queues and pointer values, can then be read. This data is used by worms and the debugger. The error signal from the network to the host indicates that one of the transputers in the network has set its error flag. This may occur, for example, on arithmetic overflow. The action occurring depends on the setting of the `HaltOnError` flag in the compiler. If it is set, the transputer will halt and the TDS will have to be reloaded. Finally, the reset is a signal from the host transputer to the network, which will reset all the processors in the network ready for loading with code.

7.1 DIY debugging using print statements

We developed most of the programs in this book without the help of a symbolic debugger (it was not available at the time, with the earlier version of the TDS). In particular, we first developed the Mandelbrot program for the network on the B004, without a physical network attached. Most of our debugging effort lay in eliminating errors in gracefully terminating the processes running on each transputer. To do this, we tested termination process by process, starting with `Controller.` When we were satisfied that was functioning correctly , we moved on to `Throughput;` and then to `Mandel.pixels; Feedback;` and so on. The following Listings show how we inserted print messages in the various processes, using the `scrstream.multiplexor` to channel the parallel outputs back for display.

```
{{{F mandelbr
-- Displays a Mandelbrot set on the screen
... LIBs, PROTOCOLs, VARs and CHANs
... SC PROC Controller
... SC PROC Mandel.pixels
... SC PROC Graphics
SEQ
  ... Input Number of rows, cols etc.
  ... Main program with debug
  ... print finished message
}}}

{{{ Main program with debug
... declarations for DEBUG multiplexor
PAR
  ... DEBUG multiplexor
  PAR
    Controller (DEBUG[1], Forward[1], Return[1], ToGraphics,
                Sc.rows, Sc.cols, No.patches, ManConst)
    Graphics (DEBUG[2], ToGraphics, No.Trans, from.filer,
              to.filer)
    PAR t = 1 FOR No.Trans
      mandel.pixels (DEBUG[t+5],
                     Forward[t], Forward[t+1], Return[t+1],
                     Return[t], t, No.Trans)
  ... HALT DEBUG
}}}

{{{ declarations for DEBUG multiplexor
VAL Mux.Size IS 100:
[Mux.Size] CHAN OF ANY DEBUG:
CHAN OF INT stopmux:
}}}

{{{ DEBUG multiplexor
scrstream.multiplexor (DEBUG, screen, stopmux)
}}}

{{{ HALT DEBUG
stopmux ! 0
}}}
```

Listing 7.1 Higher level Mandelbrot program folds, with DEBUG channels

Listing 7.1 shows the higher level Mandelbrot program folds as they were at this stage of development, with the DEBUG channels inserted into the Controller, Graphics and Mandel.pixels procedures. DEBUG is an array of channels defined in the fold declarations for DEBUG multiplexor in Listing 7.1 and we assigned DEBUG[1] to the Controller, DEBUG[2] to the Graphics and DEBUG[6] to DEBUG[8] to the Mandel.pixels processes. These channel numbers preface the screen output from the multiplexor, as in Figure 7.2. We modified the procedure declarations to include a DEBUG channel. For example:

```
PROC mandel.pixels (CHAN OF ANY DEBUG,
                    CHAN OF Coordinates FromPrev, ToNext,
                    CHAN OF Pixels FromNext, ToPrev,
                    VAL INT tran, No.Trans)
```

The procedure scrstream.multiplexor is in the library interf and must be run in parallel with the process returning output. When all output is complete, the multiplexor is switched off by sending a stop integer along the channel stopmux.

Listings 7.2 to 7.4 show some examples of how we used the DEBUG channel with write statements within the Controller, Graphics and Mandel.pixels procedures. Listing 7.2 shows monitoring of sending patches to the network in the Controller. The channel DEBUG is used in place of screen, which we formerly used with the write statements.

```
{{{ send patches
SEQ row = 1 FOR Sc.rows
  SEQ patch = 1 FOR No.patches
    {{{ send coords for this patch on this row
    INT patch.start, patch.end:
    SEQ
      patch.start := (( (patch - 1) * patch.length) + 1)
      patch.end := (patch.start + patch.length) - 1
      {{{ print row and patch
      write.full.string (DEBUG, "sending row and patch")
      write.int (DEBUG, row, 10)
      write.int (DEBUG, patch, 10)
      }}}
      ToMandels ! Coords; patch.start; patch.end; row
    }}}
}}}
```

Listing 7.2 Use of DEBUG channel in monitoring sending patches

Listing 7.3 displays monitoring more requests for work in Throughput, printing out the transputer number and the total number of processors in the network.

```
{{{
SEQ
  Mandel.Busy := FALSE
  running := TRUE
  WHILE running
    PRI ALT
      {{{ request from Mandel
      RequestMore ? Any
        SEQ
          {{{ print
          write.full.string (DEBUG,
                         "in throughput, more requested")
          write.full.string (DEBUG,
                         "transputer number & No.Trans are ")
          write.int (DEBUG, tran, 5)
          write.int (DEBUG, No.Trans, 5)
          newline (DEBUG)
          }}}
          Mandel.Busy := FALSE
      }}}
      ... input from previous
  ... COMMENT print
}}}
```

Listing 7.3 Use of DEBUG channel in monitoring requesting more patches

Finally, Listing 7.4 outputs details of the processed patches received by the graphics procedure from the network.

```
{{{ Pixels received; print them
Pixel; patch.start; patch.end; row;
No.Pixels::[Col.Its FROM 1 FOR No.Pixels]
  {{{ print
  SEQ
    {{{
    write.full.string (DEBUG, "in graphics,received pixels")
    newline(DEBUG)
    write.full.string (DEBUG, "start end row")
    write.int (DEBUG, patch.start, 5)
    write.int (DEBUG, patch.end, 5)
    write.int (DEBUG, row, 5)
    }}}
  }}}
    ... write to screen
}}}
```

Listing 7.4 Use of DEBUG channel in monitoring receiving patches

Figure 7.2 shows a brief sample output from a run of the program. `1>`, for example, indicates output from the multiplexor on channel 1 which carries information on the sending of patches to the network; and 6> output from channel 6, which gives details of the request for more work in `ThroughPut`.

```
6>in throughput, more requestedtransputer number & No.Trans are  1  3

1>sending row and patch  2  2
2>in graphics,received pixels
start end row  1  5  2  2 2 2  2  2
6>in throughput, more requestedtransputer number & No.Trans are 1  3

1>sending row and patch  2  3
2>in graphics,received pixels
start end row  6  10  2  2  2  2  2  2
6>in throughput, more requestedtransputer number & No.Trans are  1  3

1>sending row and patch  2  4
2>in graphics,received pixels
start end row  11  15  2  2  2  2  2  2
6>in throughput, more requestedtransputer number & No.Trans are  1  3

1>sending row and patch  3  1
2>in graphics,received pixels
start end row  16  20  2  2  2  2  2  2
6>in throughput, more requestedtransputer number & No.Trans are  1  3

1>sending row and patch  3  2
2>in graphics,received pixels
```

Figure 7.2 Sample output from DEBUG multiplexor

All the information was from the first processor in the network. 20 rows and columns were used as test data, with 5 patches per row containing 4 pixels each. Thus, start, end and row values of 6, 10 and 2 indicate pixels 6 to 10 on row 2; and the series of five 2s is their corresponding colour value. This output is from a program working correctly (as far as we can tell). You must be careful in interpreting the ordering of the output; the order in which the multiplexor processes its input (because of the use of the randomised `ALT`) is not necessarily the order in which it receives them. Note the `COMMENT`ed out prints in Listing 7.3; this is a quick way of suppressing output which is temporarily not required (it will, of course, involve a recompilation of the program).

By inserting such DEBUG statements judicially, you can trace the progress of the program, watching to see to which process or processor the transmitted data goes and when and how it emerges, if it does. It can be quite time consuming , particularly because of all the rebooting after the usual deadlock and the recompilation newly inserted write statements entail. A more encouraging and indispensable aid is the software debugging tool which we describe next.

7.2 Using the software debugger

This is a software tool provided with the TDS, for interactive post-mortem debugging of occam source code, running on a single transputer or on a network. To use the debugger, the program must have been halted, which may occur when the user interrupts the program as it runs by using <CONTROL><BREAK>, or when an execution error, such as overflow, occurs. Once halted you can load the debugger and then investigate the processes that were running, displaying values of variables, jumping down channels to connected processes and so on.

The next Section (7.2.1) shows how to start up the debugger; how this is done depends on whether the program is an `EXE` on the host alone, an `EXE + PROGRAM` on a network or a standalone program running via a server. Once the debugger is started, the available facilities, which are described in Section 7.2.2, are the same for all three types of program.

7.2.1 Starting up the debugger

The debugger can be used with a halted program which was previously running:

(i) on the host alone in an `EXE` fold (for example, the programs in Chapter 2 and 3);

(ii) in an `EXE` fold on the host with a `PROGRAM` fold loaded on the network (as in Chapters 4 and 5);

(ii) as a standalone program developed on the TDS, but running independently of it. This will be in a single `PROGRAM` fold, run via the afserver, as in Chapter 6.

The details of starting the debugger differ from one to the other so we shall present them in turn. A program may halt of its own accord, due to a run time error, or be interrupted while running by using <CONTROL><BREAK>. Three common causes of run time errors are:

❑ Arithmetic errors: overflow, divide by zero etc.

❑ Array out of bounds

❑ `STOP` encountered, or another process acting as though it were a `STOP`!

A `STOP` process is implemented on the transputer as though an error had occurred. This can be useful, for example, when debugging functions. Since functions can have no output processes (this is to ensure there will be no side effects – see Section 8.1.1), no print debug statements can be inserted in them. Inserting a `STOP` process in the occam code forces an error and thus allows access to the debugger. Unfortunately, it is also very easy to suffer inadvertent STOPs, when, for example, an IF or ALT construct has no TRUE guard; in particular, see the example later in this Section.

For run time errors the transputer will halt with a message indicating an error (though, frustratingly, with no details of its nature):

```
Transputer system error flag set
Press [SPACE] to reboot root transputer, [ESC] to terminate
```

The actions following run time errors can be controlled by changing the compilation error mode in the compiler options fold: in the default HALT mode, errors halt the transputer completely, no further execution being done; in STOP mode, an error stops the process in which it occurs, but allows other (parallel) processes on the same transputer to continue executing; in REDUCED mode, errors are not detected. This, of course, could be very dangerous and would only be used with a proven correct program where one might wish to avoid the overheads of run time checking.

You can also switch off the occam source code debugging facilities in the compiler options by changing the default create.debugging.info to FALSE.

Frequently a program will appear to freeze while running, with no indication of anything happening nor of an error, in which case the only recourse is to interrupt it and press the space bar to reboot the transputer. Often, the cause is deadlock.

When a transputer halts, the states of all the transputers and their memory contents are available for use with the debugger. To dump these, the TDS must first be rebooted and then the states stored in a file. The debugger can then be loaded and run. We turn now to starting up the debugger for the three types of program.

Starting the debugger with an EXE

To reboot the TDS: press space bar after the halt. Unlike a normal boot, the screen will be something like:

```
CORE DUMP FACILITY
===================
Instruction pointer at halt (absolute address) was #80000B2B
Instruction pointer at halt (rel. to start of TDS) was -940769
Options :
  c : normal core dump
  f : normal core dump + freespace
  a : standalone core dump - all of memory
  s : standalone core dump - part of memory
  any other key to skip
```

For a normal core dump: press c. This saves the states and memory contents (the a and `s` will be explained in the Section on debugging a standalone program). The next prompt is:

```
Core dump file name ("core.dmp") ?
```

and accept the default file name "core.dump" or type `another.dmp` if you prefer.

To run the debugger, autoload the debugger (either SF5 or select it from the tools), enter your `.TOP` fold to the `.EXE` fold and then run it (F6). The screen will show:

```
TDS occam 2 Debugger - V0.07 (11-May-88)
Debugging an EXE
Read Core dump file, Ignore core dump, or Quit (C,I,Q) ?
```

Select c to read the core dump file (`Ignore` will locate to an error, but you cannot then use the debug facilities); and then press return in response to:

```
Core dump filename ("core.dmp", or "QUIT") ?
```

If you interrupt a running program, the last source line executed is displayed. If the program was deadlocked, there is no last instruction and you are left at the monitor page. If an error is explicitly set, the debugger will locate to it. For example, the output in Figure 7.3 appeared when running an early version of the Mandelbrot program. We were developing it as an `EXE,` before arranging it for the network.

```
Located OK - Error explicitly set
WHILE running
  SEQ
    ALT
      ... FromNext
      ... FromLocal
    {{{ stop running?
    ... IF last transputer and no more patches, then no more
    {{{ IF no more pixels and no more patches
    IF
      (more.pixels = FALSE) AND (more.patches = FALSE)
        running := FALSE
      TRUE
        SKIP
    }}}
    }}}

  ... COMMENT print

  ToPrev ! halt
```

Figure 7.3 The occam code display for an explicit error

The cursor is left flashing on the `IF` just before the `(more.pixels = FALSE)` line. It is not clear from this what the cause of the error is; it is quite hard to spot, unless you have previously experienced it. In fact it lies in the previous `IF` fold:

```
{{{IF last transputer and no more patches, then no more
IF
  (tran = No.Trans) AND (more.from.local = FALSE)
    more.from.next := FALSE
  (tran = No.Trans) AND (more.from.local = TRUE)
    SKIP
}}}
```

where neither of the guards evaluates to `TRUE` when `tran <> No.Trans` and the `IF` consequently acts as a `STOP`. To correct this needs an extra process:

```
TRUE
  SKIP
```

should be inserted into the `IF` construct, as in Listing 6.11.

Starting the debugger with an EXE and PROGRAM running on a network

As for the `EXE` in the last Section, reboot the TDS, by pressing the space bar, and create a core dump. Now run (F6) the debugger on the `EXE` or the `PROGRAM`, if you know in which the error lies. At this stage, however, you may not know where it has occurred, so you can choose one or the other to find out. If you choose the `EXE` follow the procedure given in the last subsection and should the error be in the `PROGRAM` on the network, the debugger of course will not locate to it on the `EXE`, and so will display the monitor page (see Section 7.2.2), saying no error is set on the host transputer. In this case quit the debugger (by pressing `Q`) and rerun (F6) it on the `PROGRAM` fold. The display will be:

```
TDS occam 2 Debugger - V0.07 (11-May-88)
Debugging a PROGRAM
Transputer link, Dummy, Analyse, Host, Network dump, or Quit
                (T,D,A,H,N,Q) ?
```

Press `T` for the transputer link option (i.e. the host is connected to a network). Of the other options, `D` is for Dummy for use with a simulated network (no real one attached), and is used in conjunction with the `N`, read Network dump file option. This allows a copy of the network to be saved so that if you wish to return to debugging the program at a later date, you can avoid going through all the steps to recreate the original error, by simply reloading this saved file instead. The actual network need not be attached. `A` asserts analyse on the network i.e. this causes an analysis of the network. `H` is for use with standalone programs described in the next subsection.

Returning to the `T` option, the next prompt is:

```
Link number, or Quit (0,1,2,3,Q) ?
```

to which you type the number of the link which connects the host to the network; usually this will be the default `link2`.

To the following prompt:

```
Is host system a B004 or a B002, Ignore analyse, or Quit (4,2,I,Q) ?
```

reply `4` if you are using a B004 host (with T4 or T8 transputer). Then the screen shows the messages:

```
Reading logical name table ...
Analysing network ...
```

and will locate to the error in the occam source code, or to the monitor page if no error is set.

Starting the debugger with a standalone program

A standalone program is one developed under the TDS, but is running with its own server, for example the afserver as used with the Mandelbrot programs in Chapter 6. After the program halts (through a run time error or by interrupting with <CONTROL><BREAK>), the server terminates with a message such as:

```
Server terminated : aborted by user
```

returning you to MS-DOS.

To reboot, pressing the space bar is now inappropriate, and the usual `tds2` will not preserve the necessary data; instead you must include a `-x` option, for example:

```
tds2 -x
```

The `-x` asserts analyse so that the network is explored by the worm (see Section 7.3) which reports back the state of the processors, rather than resetting them.

You will be prompted with the core dump display, as in the `EXE` subsection above. You can create a standalone core dump file by using either the `a` or `s` options, and you must tell the system how much memory your standalone program uses. If the program uses all the memory on the host transputer, choose the `a` option, although this takes a long time to create the very large memory dump file; otherwise, if you choose the `s`, you will have to give the memory size used on the host. This creates a slight problem, because at this stage you probably do not know what it is! You can, of course, find it by opening the Configuration Information fold for the program, similar to the one in Figure 5.2, but to do this you must leave the TDS, and then add up the total amount of memory used by your program on the host: code size + workspace + vector space. To return to debugging, reboot using `tds2` with the `-x` option again (the necessary data should be still available, so you do not have to run the program again), choose the `s` option and give the size in kilobytes.

When the core dump file is written, the TDS reboots and the debugger can be run on the `PROGRAM` fold. Instead of choosing the `T` option as above, select the `H` for debugging a standalone program developed on the Host.

Having rebooted the TDS by one of the above methods, you are then ready to start debugging your program.

7.2.2 Debug facilities

Once the debugger has been started, you can commence debugging. The facilities provided with the TDS are quite extensive so we describe only those which we have found most useful. The facilities fall into two sets. The first is a high level symbolic one, dealing with occam source code which provides such features as inspection of variables and channels, by placing the cursor on them in the occam source code. The second set is geared to the assembly level where you can inspect input-output waiting on links, display the contents of the high and low priority process queues, switch from processor to processor in the network, and so on.

Symbolic debugging

The facilities provided (which can be displayed by pressing @F2) are:

1 INSPECT	display the type and value of variables etc.
2 CHANNEL	move down channel to process waiting there
3 TOP	put cursor back at error position
4 RETRACE	put cursor back to last displayed location
5 RELOCATE	put cursor back to last location line
6 INFO	display pointer information
7 R/W	toggle between read and read/write modes
8 LINKS	display the link connections
9 MONITOR	change to monitor page facilities
0 BACKTRACE	put cursor back to procedure or function call

You obtain the required facility by pressing <ALT> and the corresponding digit key. Many of the folding editor facilities are available for finding your way around the source code.

The combination of INSPECT and CHANNEL allows you to display the values of variables in one process and then jump along channels to another and display the variables in this second process. You can easily lose your bearings while doing this so the TOP key puts you back to the original error; the RETRACE reverses through the locations you have so far investigated, one by one (for example, you may have jumped down several channels); BACKTRACE takes you to the line where the current procedure or function was called.

To illustrate the use of the symbolic debugger with the `EXE` example of the last Section, when we move the cursor to `more.pixels` in Figure 7.3 and press INSPECT (@1)

```
BOOL 'more.pixels' has value TRUE (at #80000460)
```

is displayed. Similarly, by using the editor facilities, we can move to the `More pixels` fold, place the cursor on the variable `No.Pixels` and again use INSPECT to find

```
INT 'No.Pixels' has value 5 (#00000005) (at #8000044C)
{{{ More pixels
Pixel; xstart; xend; y; No.Pixels::[Col.Its FROM 1 FOR
                    No.Pixels]
  ToPrev ! Pixel; xstart; xend; y;
           No.Pixels::[Col.Its FROM 1 FOR No.Pixels]
}}}
```

We can also INSPECT channels, in a similar way:

```
CHAN 'FromNext' is empty (at #80001DB8)
{{{ FromNext
(tran <> No.Trans) & FromNext ? CASE
  ... More pixels
  ... No more pixels
}}}
```

which indicates that there is no input data waiting to be sent along this channel from the next transputer. However, the display

```
CHAN 'FromPrev' has Iptr: #80000981 and Wdesc: #800004D4
             (Hi) (at #80001DA0)
{{{ input from previous
FromPrev ? CASE
  ... coords received
  ... Receive ManConst and pass on
  ... terminate received
}}}
```

shows that there is data waiting to be sent along the channel `FromPrev` by a high priority process whose `Iptr` and `Wdesc` are as shown. These are the next instruction pointer and workspace descriptor pointer of the waiting process (see also Section 7.3).

Which process is waiting at the other end of this channel? To find out, jump down the channel by pressing CHANNEL (@2) and the display becomes:

```
Located OK
    ... Vars
    WHILE TRUE
      {{{
      SEQ
        Mandel.Busy := FALSE
        running := TRUE
        WHILE running
          PRI ALT
            {{{ request from Mandel
            RequestMore ? Any
              SEQ
                ... print
                Mandel.Busy := FALSE
            }}}
          ... input from previous
        ... COMMENT print
      }}}
```

with the cursor flashing on `RequestMore`, the other end of the channel. Once in this waiting process you can investigate further variable values and jump down other channels to waiting processes. After this, to relocate to the original error, press TOP (@3) or RETRACE (@4) process by process.

We show the use of INFO (@6) and LINKS (@8) in the example in the next subsection.

To leave the debugger, go to the monitor page (@9) and press `Q` for quit.

Monitor page

Choosing MONITOR (@9) from the symbolic level yields the display of Figure 7.4.

On the right, the memory map gives the layout in memory of workspace for variables, for the program, for any libraries linked in and for the arrays. The processor state is on the left (i.e. the values of pointers and the state of the high and low priority queues and so on). It also says that we are debugging an `EXE` on a T8 transputer, and that an error was explicitly set. The bottom line is a menu of one letter options shown in more detail in Figure 7.5.

```
TDS occam 2 Debugger - V0.07 (11-May-88)EXE (T800)

Processor State              Memory map
Iptr            #80000B6A    Workspace              : #80000070 - #80000743 ( 1748 )
Wdesc           #800003A8    Program body           : #80000744 - #8000100B ( 2248 )
IptrIntSave     #80001663    Libraries              : #8000100C - #80001A3F ( 2612 )
WdescIntSave    #8000068D    Vectorspace            : #80001A40 - #80003D1F ( 8928 )
Error           Set
FPU Error       Clear        Total memory usage     : 15536 bytes (16K)
Halt On Error   Set
Fptr1 (low      #800E63E8    On-chip memory (4K)    : #80000000 - #80000FFF
Bptr1 queue)    #800E63E8    MemStart               : #80000070
Fptr0 (high     #800005E8
Bptr0 queue)    #800005E8
TPtr1 (timer    Empty
TPtr0 queues)   Empty
Clock1 (low)    #006F81A5
Clock0 (high)   #1BE06904

Error explicitly set, Last instruction was : seterr

Option (? or [CODE INFO] for help) (A,C,D,E,H,I,L,M,N,O,P,Q,R,T,X,?) ?
```

Figure 7.4 Monitor page display corresponding to Figure 7.3

The processor states are:

`Iptr`	pointer to last instruction executed
`Wdesc`	pointer to workspace descriptor
`IptrIntSave`	pointer to low priority instruction
`WdescIntSave`	pointer to low priority workspace descriptor
`Error`	error flag set or not set
`FPU error`	FPU (on T8) error flag set or not set
`Halt on error`	halt on error flag set or not set

`Fptr1`
`Bptr1`
`Fptr0`
`Bptr0`
	pointers to Front/Back of low/high priority process queues

`TPtr1` `TPtr0`	pointers to low/high priority timer queues
`Clock0` `Clock1`	values of low/high priority clocks

`Iptr` and `Wdesc` are chiefly used with the `O` option in the menu; this is to return to the occam code at the error line located on this processor, or to the last line executed. You must supply values for `Iptr` and `Wdesc` to do this; press return to accept the default values displayed (#80000B6A and #800003A8 respectively, in this case). The screen will then show the display of Figure 7.3 again.

```
TDS occam 2 Debugger - V0.07 (11-May-88) EXE (T800)
Processor State             Help summary
Iptr            #80000B6A   A / H - Display memory as ASCII or Hex
Wdesc           #800003A8   C - Compare memory with intended code
IptrIntSave     #80001663   D - Disassemble memory
WdescIntSave    #8000068D   E - Find next processor halted on error
Error           Set         I - Inspect memory (as OCCAM types)
FPU Error       Clear       L - Display processes waiting on links
Halt On Error   Set         M - Display memory map of this processor
Fptr1 (low      #800E63E8   N - Dump network contents to file
Bptr1 queue)    #800E63E8   O / X - Display OCCAM source / Exit to OCCAM
Fptr0 (high     #800005E8   P - Change to another processor
Bptr0 queue)    #800005E8   R - Display processes on process queue
TPtr1 (timer    Empty       T - Display processes waiting on timer
TPtr0 queues)   Empty       up/down - Scroll main display
Clock1 (low)    #006F81A5   <- / -> - Scroll through processors
Clock0 (high)   #1BE06904   ? - (or [CODE INFO]) Display this help screen
Q - Quit to TDS, [REFRESH] - Redraw screen

Error explicitly set, Last instruction was : seterr

Option (? or [CODE INFO] for help) (A,C,D,E,H,I,L,M,N,O,P,Q,R,T,X,?) ?
```

Figure 7.5 The help summary of the commands

By pressing `?`, the display changes to that of Figure 7.5, giving a help summary of commands. In addition to `O` and `?` already explained above, we shall describe only `L`, `M`, `<--` , `-->` and `Q`, the others giving very low level details of memory and code which do not concern us here. In fact, while debugging an `EXE` the right and left cursor keys are not valid as they are used for scrolling through the monitor pages, processor by processor (see below). `M` returns to the memory display of Figure 7.4.

The chief use we have made of the monitor page is to show link information and to check whether an error was explicitly set, and to relocate to the occam code when a process halted. Details of empty low and high level queues are sometimes helpful (options `R` and `T`). We illustrate next with a second example, that of debugging an `EXE` with a `PROGRAM` on the network. This is the program (PARREAD) of Chapter 5 where we created a deliberate error by changing the line

```
x := (REAL32 ROUND r)
```

to

```
x := (REAL32 ROUND (r - 1))
```

This means that the first iteration on the first transputer in the network fails due to overflow because of the division by the initial estimate, `est` = 0. When the system is restarted after failure and the debugger run on the `EXE` on the host a monitor page similar to Figure 7.4 is displayed, except no error is set.

```
Location was in LIB reals, SC 1, offset 175 - Error explicitly
      set
     ... Input N and R and send on if not last transputer
     ... Number of iterations on each transputer
     SEQ r = 1 FOR R
       REAL32 x, est:
       SEQ
         Input ? CASE x.est; x; est
         SEQ itno = 1 FOR N.Its
           est := ((est + (x/est)) * Half)
         Output ! x.est; x; est
  }}}
:
}}}
...F code
...F descriptor
...F link
...F debug
...F CODE SC Iterations
}}}
```

Figure 7.6 occam code illustrating overflow error

Leaving this and running the debugger on the `PROGRAM` fold results in the source code display of Figure 7.6 (not the monitor page, since error is set), with the cursor flashing on the line `est := ((est + (x/est)) * Half)`. The message at the top of the screen indicates that the processor was executing a real arithmetic library routine and that error was definitely found. To find which transputer is involved we press INFO @6 and the display shows:

```
Located to Iptr #8150, and Wdesc #8081, (Lo pri), Processor 1 (T212)
```

which says that the error was in a low priority process on the first transputer in the network. Now, if we did not know the cause of the mistake, we could investigate the value of the variable `est` by placing the cursor on it and using @1:

```
REAL32 'est' has value 0.0 (#00000000) (at #8092)
```

We could investigate further by displaying the monitor page for this processor, as in Figure 7.7, overleaf:

```
TDS occam 2 Debugger - V0.07 (11-May-88)        Processor 1 (T212)
Processor State              Memory map
Iptr            #8233        Workspace          : #8032 - #80B1 ( 128 )
Wdesc           #8051        Configuration code : #80B2 - #80C3 ( 18 )
IptrIntSave                  Program body       : #80C4 - #8183 ( 192 )
WdescIntSave                 Libraries          : #8184 - #87CF ( 1612 )
Error           Set
Halt On Error   Set          Total memory usage : 2000 bytes
Fptr1 (low      Empty
Bptr1 queue)                 On-chip memory (2K) : #8000 - #87FF
Fptr0 (high     Empty        MemStart           : #8024
Bptr0 queue)
TPtr1 (timer    Empty        Debugger has enough memory for 758 processors
TPtr0 queues)   Empty
Clock1 (low)    #5964
Clock0 (high)   #592B

Error explicitly set, Last instruction was : seterr

Option (? or [CODE INFO] for help) (A,C,D,E,H,I,L,M,N,O,P,Q,R,T,X,?) ?
```

Figure 7.7 Monitor page for Processor 1; error is caused by overflow.

We see from this that the error was set on this T2 transputer, processor 1, and that the low and high priority queues were empty. Now, by pressing the right arrow key -->, we can move to the monitor page of the next transputer in the network, and pressing `L` will give the link information for that processor as in Figure 7.8.

```
TDS occam 2 Debugger - V0.07 (11-May-88)        Processor 2 (T212)

Processor State              Link information
Iptr            #812D        Link 0 out Empty
Wdesc           Invalid      Link 1 out Empty
IptrIntSave                  Link 2 out Empty
WdescIntSave                 Link 3 out Empty
Error           Clear        Link 0 in Iptr: #812E Wdesc: #8081 (Lo)
Halt On Error   Set          Link 1 in Empty
Fptr1 (low      Empty        Link 2 in Empty
Bptr1 queue)                 Link 3 in Empty
Fptr0 (high     Empty        Event in Empty
Bptr0 queue)
TPtr1 (timer    Empty        Link 0 connected to Processor 1, Link 1
TPtr0 queues)   Empty        Link 1 connected to Processor 3, Link 0
Clock1 (low)    #5AA2        Link 2 not connected
Clock0 (high)   #A879        Link 3 not connected

Booted from link 0

Error not set, Last instruction was : in

Option (? or [CODE INFO] for help) (A,C,D,E,H,I,L,M,N,O,P,Q,R,T,X,?) ?
```

Figure 7.8 Monitor page for Processor 2, showing link data.

From this we see that error was not set on this processor. We cannot return to the occam source as the `Wdesc` is invalid, which means that no process was running on this processor. The link information shows that none was waiting for communication, with the exception of `link0in,` which is connected to link1 of processor 1. Link1 of this processor is connected to link0 of the next (3). When we look at processor 3 we find a display the same as this. The implication is that processor 1 had done some calculation, but 2 and 3 probably had not started; this narrows the error to lie before data was sent to processor 2.

To quit the monitor page, press `Q`.

7.3 Worms

A worm is another software tool, a program that probes its way along channels from transputer to transputer, reporting back what it finds as it goes. It is used to test the state of a network – for example, that the physical network corresponds precisely to its description in the application program that is designed to run on it. Failure to load a program might occur if they did differ through, say, the program being configured for T4 transputers while the net consists of T2s, or if the links are incorrectly connected or some of them are missing. Worms also check the hardware of the network is working properly. We have experienced several such problems when, for example, for no apparent reason other than presumably a poor connection, the return link in the Newton-Raphson program of Chapter 5 fails. In fact, on occasions, we have been unable to load a network with the Mandelbrot program, again for no apparent reason. However, we "flushed" away the problem by loading the network with the Application program of Chapter 4 and then reloading the Mandelbrot one!

For the first of these failures, checking the links using the debugger will lead you to a disconnected link (the display will be `CHAN 'PipeN' is empty (PLACED AT 7) (Link 3 in) (Unconnected) )` , so the worm is not essential here. However, to illustrate use of the worm, after loading the network, we simulate a poor connection by physically removing a link!

7.3.1 How a worm works

The worm algorithm is described in Miller (1987), 'Exploring multiple transputer arrays'. The worm program is run as an `EXE` on the host and squirts itself into the network down the link of the host connecting it to the network. It explores each transputer in turn, deducing the type from the time taken to execute a standard loop of code. By sending some probing data through each link in turn (in order 2, 3, 0, 1), the worm finds which links are connected, by waiting for the return of an answer within a fixed time. If there is no reply, the link is unconnected; if the data returned is incorrect, a fault is assumed on that link. The worm also checks memory, if requested, and the analyse, reset and error lines. It then sends a copy of itself to another transputer in the network and performs the tests on this one.

7.3.2 Running the worm

The worm is found in the TDS tools fold and is loaded as usual by pressing F5 on the network tester fold. Then exit to your PROGRAM fold and run the worm (F6). This will match results against your own network definition as given in your PROGRAM CONFIG INFO fold (provided you created one, of course; if you did not, the worm will still try to match but use its own numbering scheme for processors and links etc.). Immediately after running the worm, the screen display will be:

```
Please select mode :-
  Check T4/T8 network (using internal ram)        (A)
  Check T2 network (using internal ram)           (B)
  Check mixed T2/M2/T4/T8 network (requires 6k)   (C)
  Test T4/T8 network                              (4)
  Test T2 network                                 (2)
  or Quit                                         (Q)  ?
```

and you select the appropriate mode for either checking or testing transputers of word length 16-bits or 32-bits. "Checking" means a network is explored, the screen output being loading data as in Figure 7.9, but not tested, thereby consuming less memory (2 Kbytes / transputer of internal memory). The mixed option requires 6 Kbytes of memory and checks networks of transputers with different word lengths.

If a test option (either 2 or 4) is chosen, the display is:

```
What type of test :-
  Develop and Debug (Alter test defaults)         (D)
  Flash error lights                              (E)
  Full memory (with pauses) and link test         (F)
  Link only test                                  (L)
  Memory only test (no pauses)                    (M)
  or Quit                                         (Q)  ?
```

Develop and debug allows you to alter certain test defaults such as the amount of memory to be tested on each transputer. Flashing error lights allows progress of the worm to be followed, so that if it stops for an error, you can see on which transputer it is. Full testing produces output such as in Figure 7.10 below. The worm tests all memory encountered on each transputer, with a time delay to allow you to send the data to a file , if you wish; it also tests all links in the network. If this option is chosen the display is:

```
Which link (0, 1, 2, or 3) to try squirting worm
(Warning: avoid the host transputer's boot link!) ?
```

and choose link2 the default link from the host to the network (the host's boot link is link0 to the IBM PC). Then follows:

```
Full (F) or brief (B) results ?
```

On our system the choice B sometime gives:

```
Option B Selected
t
The total number of transputers found is 1
Testing network ...
Hardware error found - please repeat with full display
Missing transputer 1
Testing will repeat - type <any> to exit
```

This error arises because of an untraced defect we have on our particular B006 board. After running a program we have to press the reset button on the B006 before we can reload the program or run the tester successfully. In this case, the worm reports a hardware error, a missing transputer!

When left for six seconds the testing is repeated. After resetting the B006 and rerunning the tester the display shows

```
Option B Selected
ttttt
The total number of transputers found is 5
Testing network ...
Hardware error found - please repeat with full display
Missing transputer 4
Testing will repeat - type <any> to exit
```

where, of course, transputer 4 is not found because we removed the link! (By now, we had purchased another T2 transputer for the B006). The line of `ttttt` denotes the number of transputers and appear one by one as each is tested.

If, instead of the brief option, we choose the full one, the displays are as in Figures 7.9 and 7.10. Figure 7.9 gives loading data of the network, processor by processor. `MT*` refers to the master transputer (the host in this case) and the `Id` otherwise refers to the numbering of the processors given in the `PROGRAM`. A `*` indicates the worms own numbering which it produces if the `PROGRAM CONFIG INFO` does not exist or if it does not match the physical network. Hence, the reason for `3*` here is that the configuration data was out of date; we had created it for a network of three T2 transputers, when, in fact, there were four of them. The boot link is the link through which the worm booted the transputer, and is not necessarily the same as that used when booting the `PROGRAM`. The fourth T2 (the connecting cable from the third transputer was removed, remember) was booted via link3, which is hard wired on a B004 board to link2 of its neighbour (see Section 4.5.2). The `Booted by` columns indicate which parent booted the transputer; for example, the host (`MT*`), via its link2, booted the first T2 transputer (`Id` = 1); and it, in turn, via link1, booted the second T2 transputer (`Id` = 2); and so on.

```
T2 Full Test
Loading and matching network ...

       Boot Booted by                        Analysed    Error
Id     Link Id      Link  Type   Speed  or Reset    Line
--     ---- --      ----  ----   -----  --------    -----
MT*    --   --      --    Host   ---    Analysed    Not clear
1      0    MT*     2     T212a  -17       ok       ok      ......
2      0    1       1     T212a  -20 Anlsd not Resetok      ......
3      0    2       1     T212a  -20       ok       ok      ......
3*     3    3       2     T212a  -20       ok       ok

The total number of transputers found is  5
```

Figure 7.9 Loading data of a network.

The speed of the transputer is given in Mhz. The `Not clear` for the error line on the master appears when the worm is run for the first time. The `Anlsd not Reset` on processor 2 may indicate a fault in the reset/analyse chain. Finally, each row of dots indicates memory being tested.

After the loading data, a second worm investigates memory and network connections which are then returned and displayed as in Figure 7.10. The amount of memory tested is shown for each processor.

```
Testing network ...

              Memory    Link: 0         1          2         3
Id Type   Tested Error   Id Link   Id Link    Id Link  Id Link
-- ----   ------ -----   -- ----   -- ----    -- ----  -- ----
MT*Host     --     --     ----      ----       1  0      ----
1  T212a    --     --     MT*2      2  0       oooo      oooo
2  T212a    10 k   ok     1  1      3  0       oooo      oooo
3  T212a    10 k   ok     2  1      oooo       3* 3      oooo
3* T212a    10 k   ok     oooo      oooo       oooo      3  2

Missing transputer 4
Testing will repeat - type <any> to exit
```

Figure 7.10 Memory test data and link connections of a network.

The first one in a T2 network stores the worm (10 Kbytes) and so is not tested. In this example there is no memory error. The remainder of the display shows the processor interconnections. There are four columns corresponding to the four links of each transputer. An entry `----` indicates that the link was not tried (for example, on the host); `oooo` shows an unattached link; and `T L` means the link is connected to link `L` of transputer `T`. Thus, link0 of processor 2 is connected to link1 of processor 1; and, link1 of processor 2 is connected to link0 of processor 3; and, its other links are not connected. Similarly, we can see that link1 of processor 3 is not connected to processor 4, as we expected. This is confirmed by the missing transputer message. link3 of 3* is hard wired to processor 3, as we noted above.

8

Some further topics

8.1 Further occam

There are several features of occam which we have not used in our programs, such as functions and the `CASE` process; we present these and a few smaller topics in this Section.

8.1.1 Functions

The compiler ensures that occam functions can have no side-effects; that is, it is syntactically incorrect to write code that would change the results of variables in scope, other than those used for returning the value of the function. Unlike in Pascal, a function may also return several results. For example, to find the maximum and minimum of a set of values `x[n]` we could use Listing 8.1 on the following page.

The function body is introduced by the `VALOF` construct; this is followed by whatever calculations are necessary; and the function is ended by returning the values using `RESULT`. In this present case, two results in the variables `Max` and `Min` are returned. Note, these variables are declared within the function (on the second line), and that, to correspond, the `FUNCTION` line indicates that the type of the returned variables is `REAL32, REAL32`. Note also, again unlike Pascal, the name of the function is NOT the name of the returned variable – clearly, when there is more than one returned variable this is impossible. Finally, note the alignment of `RESULT` and the last "`:`".

Restrictions within a `VALOF` preclude the use of `PAR`, `ALT` and channels; and assignments can only be to variables within the `VALOF` or just prior to it. These remove the possibility of side effects, but also mean, for example, that print statements cannot be included when debugging functions. Instead, you can force a `STOP` in a function (by including a `STOP` process) and then using the TDS debugger, as described in Section 7.2.

```
REAL32, REAL32 FUNCTION MaxMin (VAL [] REAL32 x, VAL INT N)

  REAL32 Max, Min:

  VALOF
    SEQ
      Max, Min := x[0], x[0]

      SEQ n = 1 FOR N-1
        SEQ

          IF
            Max > x[n]
              Max := x[n]
            TRUE
              SKIP

          IF
            Min < x[n]
              Min := x[n]
            TRUE
              SKIP

    RESULT Max, Min

:

  Maxn, Minn := MaxMin (x, N)
```

Listing 8.1 Function for finding a maximum and minimum value

8.1.2 *CASE*

There is a `CASE` process (not to be confused with the `CASE` for use with `PROTOCOLs` seen in Chapters 5 and 6) which is very similar to the `CASE` selection mechanism in Pascal. An example is shown on the next page, where `p`, `q`, `r` and `s` are processes. Note the usual indentation conventions. `ELSE` (which cannot be used with `IF`) is optional, and is the catch-all category. Without an `ELSE`, if the `CASE` selection `a + b` did not evaluate to 1, 2 or 3, the `CASE` would act as a `STOP`. The selector must be of type `INT`.

```
CASE a + b

  1
    p
  2
    q
  3
    r
  ELSE
    s
```

8.1.3 Other occam

There are 6 bit-wise operators:

```
p/\q -- AND            p><q -- Exclusive OR
p/\q -- OR             p>>5 -- shift p right 5 places
~p   -- NOT            p<<3 -- shift p left 3 places
```

`ALT` guards may also have Booleans attached. For example,

```
x > y & From.App ? A
```

will only input from `From.App` when `x > y` is `TRUE,` and the channel `From.App` is ready. Note the use of "`&`". `A special form involves a Boolean and SKIP` (i.e. no input!)

```
ALT
  cold & SKIP                 -- may be chosen if cold
    ... first alternative     -- is TRUE when ALT started

  ... some other alternative
```

In fact, a further special case is `TRUE & SKIP` which is always ready; this is usually used with `PRI ALT`, as the last alternative in the list. This guarantees that when a rare but important message arrives on an input channel it will be noticed:

```
WHILE running
  PRI ALT
    finish ? any
      running := FALSE
    TRUE & SKIP
      ... main part
```

Without the `PRI,` the `TRUE & SKIP` might be taken at every repeat of the `WHILE,` with the `finish` channel being ignored.

8.2 Correctness of occam programs

Occam is closely based on CSP (Communicating Sequential Processes – Hoare (1978)) and has formally defined semantics. Programs written in it could thus be formally specified and verified. Further, formal techniques enable program transformations, so that, for example, an inefficient, understandable version could be changed into an equivalent, more efficient but probably less readable one. Burns (1988) investigates transformations in some detail and Goldsmith (1988) has produced a package to automate this.

8.3 Load balancing and monitoring of parallel programs

Load balancing is the task of spreading the computational load of the program amongst the processors of a network so that they are all kept as busy as possible. This is not a trivial task. In Chapter 5, we saw how this could be done for a pipeline and derived some theoretical results for processing time which quite closely approximated the actual timings. In Chapter 6, we tried the same for a processor farm, in particular for the Mandelbrot algorithm distributed over several processors. We derived some theoretical approximations, but made several simplifying assumptions on the way; for example, we assumed that external memory with its longer access time, was not used (in fact, the program code is so large that external memory must be used , as could be seen from the CONFIG INFO fold for the Mandelbrot program). We also assumed an average value for the number of times the WHILE loop was performed in the algorithm, since it is not possible in general to calculate this. We concluded that, with T8 transputers, some buffering of data would be desirable but did not investigate this further.

One reason is that it becomes increasingly difficult to analyse the behaviour of a network theoretically. With several T8s the first transputer would be mostly message passing all the time and not doing much computation; this changes the conditions of our analysis (that the first transputer does about ~1/M of the total computation). Adding buffers also complicates this approach. Nevertheless, we would like to know how busy the processors in our network are, at any time during the running of the program, to find where the program is spending its time, to identify any bottle-necks and to see the usefulness of buffers and so on. We would like to profile or monitor all the processors to investigate the ratio of communications to computation.

Several authors have developed such tools to monitor:

❑ processor usage (idle time monitoring)

❑ link usage (actual traffic compared to peak capacity)

❑ profiling of code (how often certain parts are executed)

An example of a profiling system is GRAIL – Graphical Representation of Activity, Interconnection and Loading – developed by GEC Research (Stepney, 1988), which, after the program has finished executing, displays processor usage and overall code usage in a colour display. This highlights "hot" and "cold" lines of occam code, using displays of processes similar to, but more elaborate than, the one in Figure 6.7 so that the parallel structures and the inter-communications are clear. Other parts of a program can be displayed similarly by entering folds, using an interactive menu.

Henderson (1989) describes a simple idle-time monitor for networks called TDM (Transputer Development Monitor). This is an additional process which runs in parallel with the application program, monitoring its operation. It does this by measuring the unused processor time, during which the processor is idle. A major problem in designing monitors is that they may interfere with the actual running of the application program on the network – an occam manifestation of the Heisenberg effect; for example, in returning data from individual processors for display or in obtaining the data in the first place. Clearly, this interference must be kept to a minimum. In TDM, to save passing monitoring data along the links of the running program, it is stored in the memory of the processor during execution, and then passed for display after completion of execution of the application. The monitoring process simply counts idle processor cycles, until it is interrupted by another process which has some genuine work to do. This it achieves by the following occam code:

```
WHILE running
  PRI ALT
    ... terminate?
    ... report idle count when requested
    TRUE & SKIP -- count idle cycles
      SEQ
        cycles := cycles + 1
        PAR
          SKIP -- if another process is ready let it interrupt
          SKIP
```

After the run is complete, the CPU usage against time may be displayed graphically. From this one can see when the processors are busy, when they are idling.

8.4 Occam versus other comers

Reluctance to program in occam arises for several reasons: for instance, an already high investment in existing Fortran or C programs; or the difficulty of learning and using occam. The thinking is that it is easier to manually "parallelise" existing Fortran programs using one of the several "alien" compilers written for the transputer.

However, the presumed difficulties with occam are largely non-existent and the actual hard parts will occur using an alien language, in any case. Occam, as its name suggests and its developers intended, is a simple language to learn and use, especially if you are already fluent in programming in Pascal or Fortran etc; the differences are essentially constructs such as `ALT` and `PAR`. The "difficulties" we have found were not in the developing of algorithms in occam, but, for example, in arranging and configuring programs to run on a network of transputers; for instance, the `Throughput` and `Feedback` mechanism to route data; and in programming (or rather debugging) the graceful close down of processes. However, all those aspects or their equivalent must still be faced in a concurrent version of Fortran or other such language; at present, they cannot be easily avoided. The development of software to handle concurrency automatically is still very much in its infancy, and it may be some time before substantial progress is made in this area.

8.5 Further parallel methods

The pipeline we discussed in Chapters 1 to 5 is a particular case of algorithmic parallelism, in which each processor carries out part of the algorithm, then passes on the (processed) data to the next processor. It is also known as a dataflow decomposition. A compiler, in which the lexer continually accepts characters and passes tokens to the parser, which then passes its data to the code generator, is another example.

In the processor farm of Chapter 6, which is also known as independent tasks or event parallelism, each processor executes the same code independently of all other processors.

Another form we have not demonstrated is geometric parallelism or data structure decomposition, in which each processor executes the same code but on a different set of data corresponding to a different area of the system being simulated. Processors require boundary data from their neighbours. Examples are image processing, where the image is split into distinct areas for processing.

Table 8.1 summarises some of the major properties that typify each of these approaches. The entries are not necessarily precise statements; for example, memory requirements for the pipeline are given as low. Clearly this depends on the problem, but compared to implementing the program on a farm (when this is possible) the amount of code will be smaller.

These examples are given as illustrations; other forms of parallelism are clearly possible, including, for example, hybrids of pipelines, processor farms or geometric parallelism. More details can be found in Bowler et al (1989) and in the INMOS technical notes (1988).

Table 8.1 Major properties of approaches to parallelism

Type of parallelism	**Data Handling**	**Nature of program on each processor**	**Memory requirement**	**Communication**
Algorithmic, pipeline, data flow decomposition.	Processed data passed on.	Could be same, could be different.	Low.	Could be high (problem dependent)
Independent task, event, processor farm.	Different data on each processor, farmed out by controller.	Independent of other processors. Same code on each.	Sizable.	Routing of data to and from controller needed.
Geometric, data structure decomposition.	Subsets of total data on each processor.	Dependent on data from other processors. Same code on each.	Less (has subset of total data).	higher (need to access data on other processors).

Appendix A

Glossary

Alien File Server
An historical name for the Host File Server.

Alien language
A language other than occam (such as C, Pascal or Fortran) which is embedded in an occam program.

Allocation (PLACE)
Allocation places a variable, channel, timer, array or port at an absolute location in the transputer's memory.

```
PLACE FromServer AT link2out:
```

Alternation (ALT)
Alternation combines a number of processes guarded by inputs, and performs the input associated with the input that is ready.

```
ALT
  C1 ? x
    C3 ! x
  C2 ? x
    C3 ! x
```

Alternative
A component of an alternation.

Analyse
A signal to a transputer to tell it to halt at the next descheduling point to allow the state of the processor to be read. Used by the worms and the debugger to find the state of the processors in a network.

Bitwise operation
Operation on the individual bits in the representation of a value.

Board
One of a number of INMOS boards containing one or more transputers which can be linked together to form networks.

```
B004, B006 etc.
```

CASE input
Selects the protocol of an input on a single channel with variant protocol.

```
FromMandels ? CASE
  Pixel; start; end; row
    ToGraphics ! start; end; row
  halt
    running := FALSE
```

Channel
Unbuffered, uni-directional point-to-point connection for communication between two processes running in parallel.

Channel protocol
The format of communication on a channel.

Communication
The communication of data between concurrent processes.

Configuration
Configuration associates the components of a program with a set of physical resources; usually this is allocating occam processes to processors in a network, and channels to links. The term is used in three ways: making the allocation decision in a program; the occam code describing the allocations; and, applying the compiler to the occam description.

```
PLACED PAR m = 1 FOR M
  PROCESSOR m T2
    PLACE Pipe0 AT linkin:
    PLACE Pipe1 At linkout:
    It(Pipe0, Pipe1)
```

Configurer
A TDS utility which when run on a `PROGRAM` fold generates the information needed to control the distribution of processes to processors.

Construction

A construction combines processes. occam processes are built from simpler processes. Constructions are: `SEQ, IF, CASE, WHILE, PAR` and `ALT.`

Deadlock

The state of a program when two or more concurrent processes can no longer continue to execute, because each is waiting for the others to communicate.

Definition

A definition introduces a `PROTCOL,` a `PROC`, a `FUNCTION` or a `RETYPES.`

Descheduling point

A point in an executing program at which a process may be suspended, for example, to wait for communication or after its allocated share of processor time. Descheduling points are instructions such as jumps, loop ends, `ALT` waits etc.

Error modes

A program can be compiled in one of three optional error modes: `HALT, STOP` or `REDUCED.` The mode determines what happens when a program error, such as overflow or array bound violation, occurs.

Error signal

A signal from a transputer to indicate that an error has occurred in a running program. Usually relayed to the Host, so it can report the error and allow the debugger to be run, if desired.

EXE

An `EXE` compilation fold contains occam code designed to run within the TDS. An `EXE` is a complete, executable program.

Extraction

the same as linking, used in the context of `SC` and `PROGRAM` folds.

Filed fold

A fold whose contents are saved in a separate file in the filing system.

Fold

In the folding editor, a fold contains a block of lines, which may themselves contain further nested folds. The folds can be opened to display the contents, or closed, in which case they are replaced by a single marker line called a fold line.

```
... This is a fold with contents not displayed
```

Folds can be used by the TDS for storing data, for example, compiled occam code.

Foldset

A fold produced by the TDS after a program is compiled containing a sequence of nested folds such as compiled occam code, linking data, etc.

Guard

Guards are used to avoid specific communications in an `ALT` constructor. They can be an `input`, a `Boolean & input` or a `Boolean & SKIP`.

```
M > N & C1 ? number1
```

Hard channels

Channels mapped onto (some of) a transputer's links (contrast Soft Channels).

Host

Used in two ways:
(i) the (micro)computer which is running the server to the TDS.
(ii) the combination of the (micro)computer and the transputer running the TDS.

Host File Server

A file server which provides access to the filing system and terminal I/O of a host operating system, which is used when using a standalone program. Also known as Alien File Server.

Indentation

An offset from the left hand edge. Indentation must be an even number. In occam indentation is critical, since it is used to delimit the extent of processes etc.

Input

An input receives a value along a named channel and assigns the value to a variable.

```
keyboard ? Any
```

Instance

Similar to the call of a procedure in other languages.

Library (LIB)

There are two types:
(i) a collection of text folds containing constants and `PROTOCOL` definitions
(ii) `SC` folds containing procedure and function definitions.

Libraries may be shared between parts of a program, or between different programs.

Link

(i) As hardware, a link is the serial communication between two transputers.
(ii) In program compilation, to link is to collect together all the code for a compilation unit and put it into a single filed fold.

Livelock

A state of the program where a process remains active but does no useful processing. For example, it behaves like the infinite loop:

```
WHILE TRUE
  SKIP
```

Loader

A TDS facility which loads and distributes a compiled occam program (in a `PROGRAM` fold) onto a transputer network.

Network

A network consists of a number of transputers connected via (some of) their links.

Output

An output sends the value of an expression along a named channel.

```
Pipe0 ! x + y
```

Parallel process

A parallel process (`PAR`) is one whose component processes are executed in parallel.

Placement

A configuration statement which places a process at a particular memory address.

```
PLACE Pipe0 AT link2in:
```

Priority

Priority can be given to a `PAR` or an `ALT` constuction. Parallel processes can have two levels of priority "high" and "low". There are two process queues corresponding to each priority level. High priority ones can pre-empt low level ones. High priority is often used to give communications precedence. With an `ALT`, high priority ensures that the first alternative is "noticed", that is dealt with whenever it is ready.

PROGRAM

A `PROGRAM` compilation fold containing occam code which is to be loaded and run on a network.

Protocol
The format and type of values passed along a channel.

Reset signal
A reset signal is a transputer initialisation control signal.

Root transputer
The transputer in a network connected to the host computer.

Retyping
Retyping is changing the data type of a bit pattern, from one data type to another.

SC
An `SC` is a compilation fold, known as a seperate compilation unit, which is not a complete program in itself, but contains one or more procedures or functions. Used to load different `SCs` on different processors in a network, and to avoid recompilation of units which have not changed since the last compilation.

Scope
The range of definition of a named object, such as a variable; it is the range of definition of the following process, its extent being delineated by the indentation.

Segment
A segment is one or more components of an array.

Sequential process
A sequential process `(SEQ)` is a process whose component processes are executed in sequence.

Server
A program (often written in C) running on a host (micro)computer connected to a transputer network, which provides access to the filing system and terminal I/O of the host computer. The server normally boots up the network as well.

SKIP
A primitive process which starts, performs no action and then terminates immediately. It is a null process and is used with certain syntactical forms if no action is required.

Soft channels
''Software'' channels declared and used between processes running on a single transputer. Used in contrast to ''Hard Channels''.

Specification
A specification is a declaration, an abbreviation or a definition and specifies a name which may be used within the associated scope.

```
INT x: -- specification
SEQ
  x := 5
  ... etc.
```

Standalone program
An occam program running outside the TDS, ususally booted onto a transputer network from a host computer, and supported for I/O etc. by a server running on the host. The program will usually have been developed using the TDS.

STOP
A primitive process which starts, performs no action and does not terminate. Usually used to stop a program running so that some debugging investigation can be done.

Subsystem
In a transputer board architecture, the combination of the Reset, Analyse and Error signals which allow the board to control another board of transputers.

Tag
An identifier of a protocol variant specified in a variant protocol definition.

TDS
The transputer development system, consists of a plug-in board containing at least one transputer and the development software which runs on the board. Used to develop occam programs. Contains a folding editor, a compiler, file handler, debugger, and several software tools.

Timer
A timer is a clock which can be accessed by any number of concurrent processes.

Tools
A suite of software tools provided with the TDS, contained in a Toolkit fold, to aid in program development and network testing.

Variant protocol
A variant protocol specifies a list of possible protocols for communication on a single channel.

Vector space
The memory used to store array variables in an occam program.

Worm

A software tools program that distributes itself through a network of transputers to allow the network to be loaded, tested or analysed. Used, for example, to test the integrity of links and memory of the processors, and to analyse a halted system so the debugger can be used.

Workspace

The memory used to store scalar variables in an occam program.

Appendix B

Bibliography

The individual INMOS technical notes contain a wealth of information, and have been published as two collections in *Communicating Process Architectures* and *Transputer Technical Notes,* by Prentice Hall (1988). Prentice Hall have also published *Transputer Development System* (1988), a reference manual to the TDS, and *The Transputer DataBook* (1988), a bible on the transputer family architecture.

The Occam User's Group also hold Conferences twice a year. The Proceedings, published by IOS, Amsterdam, are a very valuable source of up-to-date papers on occam programs and transputer applications.

Further sources produced by the SERC/DTI Transputer Initiative are their bi-monthly *Mailshot* and less frequent *Loan Reports*, available from The Transputer Coordination Team, Rutherford Appleton Laboratory, G54, Building R1, Chilton, Didcot, Oxon, OX11 0QX.

References

Atkin P, Performance Maximisation, *INMOS Technical Note 17,* INMOS, (1987)

This is also in *Transputer Technical Notes,* Prentice Hall (1988)

Brookes G R and Stewart A J, *Introduction to occam 2 on the Transputer*, MacMillan Computer Science Series, London, (1989).

Burns A, *Programming in occam 2* , Addison-Wesley,, Workingham (1988).

CODE (C-DAC occam Development Environment) User's Manual, Centre for Development of Advanced Software, Pune, India (1989).

Henderson B, A Simple Idle-Time Monitor for Transputer Networks, *SERC / DTI Transputer Initiative MAILSHOT* , Rutherford Appleton Laboratory, (Oct 1989) pp 67- 76.

INMOS Limited, *Occam 2 Reference Manual,* Prentice-Hall, London, (1988).

INMOS Limited, *Transputer Development System,* Prentice-Hall, London, (1988).

Jones G and Goldsmith M, *Programming in occam 2,* Prentice-Hall, (1988).

Kerridge J, *Occam Programming: a Practical Approach,* Blackwell Scientific Publications, (1987).

Miller N, Exploring Multiple Transputer Arrays, *INMOS Technical Note 21,* INMOS, (1987).

Packer J, Exploiting Concurrency: A Ray Tracing Example, *INMOS Technical Note 7,* INMOS, (1987).

This is also in *Communicating Process Architecture*, Prentice Hall, (1988)

Pountain D and May D, *A Tutorial Introduction to Occam Programming*, London, Blackwell Scientific Publications, (1987).

Stepney S, GRAIL - Graphical Representation of Activity, Interconnection and Loading, in *Parallel Programming of Transputer Based Machines* (Ed. Muntean T) OUG-7, Proceedings of the 7th occam user's group, Grenoble, IOS Amsterdam, (1988). pp 272-280

Wayman R, Transputer Development Systems, in *Transputer Applications,* (Ed. Harp G), Pitman (1989) pp. 31- 82.

Wexler J, *Concurrent programming in occam 2,* Ellis Horwood, (1989).

Appendix C

The syntax of occam2

The first part of this appendix is a top down description of the syntax of occam2, along with some cross-references and snatches of occam examples to illustrate the nearby syntax. The second section is an alphabetic index to the sections of the main body of the appendix. The final part is a list of occam reserved words, again with a reference to the appropriate section of the Appendix.

Notation

The meaning of

```
process        = SKIP
                 | STOP
                 | action            :=, ?, !
```

is "A process is a SKIP or a STOP or an action", etc. The "`:=, ?, !`" are some examples of actions.

{ process } means "a list of zero or more processes on separate lines".

{0, expression } means "a list of zero or more expressions separated from one another by ,".

{1 ; input.item} means "a list of one or more input items separated from one another by ;".

<1, 2> is a cross reference to sections C.1 and C.2 of this appendix. The absence of such a reference usually indicates the explanation is nearby in the same section.

C.1 Processes

```
process          =    SKIP
                 |    STOP
                 |    action                      :=, ?, !
                 |    construction <2>            SEQ, IF, CASE, WHILE, PAR, ALT
                 |    instance     <13>           Application(To.App, From.App)
```

STOP starts but never proceeds and never terminates. SKIP starts, performs no action and terminates.

```
action           =    assignment                  est := x * half
                 |    input                       keyboard ? Any
                 |    output                      Pipe0 ! x

assignment       =    variable := expression
                 |    variable.list := expression.list

                                                  X, Y := Zero32, Zero32

variable.list    =    {1 , variable}    <9>

expression.list  =    {1 , expression} <10>

input            =    channel ? variable
```

An input inputs a value from the channel, assigns it to the variable and then terminates.

```
output           =    channel ! expression
```

An output evaluates the expression, outputs the result to the channel, then terminates.

C.2 Construction

```
construction     =    sequence
                 |    conditional
                 |    selection
                 |    loop
                 |    parallel
                 |    alternation

sequence         =    SEQ                         SEQ
                        { process }   <1>           x := R
                                                    y := z
```

Each process starts only when its predecessor terminates (if it does).

```
conditional      =    IF                          IF
                        { choice }                  ch = stopch
                                                      running := FALSE
choice           =    guarded.choice                ch <> stopch
                 |    conditional                     SKIP
```

```
guarded.choice   =   boolean
                       process  <1>

boolean          =   expression <10>

selection        =   CASE selector
                       { option }

option           =   {1 , case.expression}
                       process  <1>
                   | ELSE
                       process

selector         =   expression <10>

case.expression  =   expression
```

```
CASE a + b
  1
    p
  2
    q
  3
    r
  ELSE
    s
```

```
loop             =   WHILE boolean
                       process

parallel         =   PAR
                       { process }
```

```
WHILE running
  PAR
    echo   ! ch
    To.App ! ch
```

```
alternation      =   ALT
                       { alternative }

alternative      =   guarded.alternative
                   | alternation

guarded.
alternative      =   guard
                       process

guard            =   input <1>
                   | boolean & input
                   | boolean & SKIP
```

```
ALT
  RequestMore ? Any
    Busy := FALSE
  FromPrev  ? start
    ToLocal ! start
```

C.3 Replicator

```
sequence         =   SEQ replicator
                       process <1>

conditional      =   IF replicator
                       choice <2>

parallel         =   PAR replicator
                       process

alternation      =   ALT replicator
                       alternative
```

```
SEQ r = 1 FOR R
  SEQ
    x   := r
    est := x + 1
```

```
replicator       =     name = base FOR count

base             =     expression <10>

count            =     expression
```

C.4 Types

```
Type             =     primitive.type
                     | array.type                [255] INT Col.Its

primitive.type   =     CHAN OF protocol <7>
                     | TIMER
                     | BOOL
                     | BYTE
                     | INT
                     | INT16
                     | INT32
                     | INT64
                     | REAL32
                     | REAL64

array.type       =     [ expression ] type       [M+1] CHAN OF Pixels Return
```

C.5 Literal

```
literal          =     integer                   15
                     | byte                      'A'
                     | integer(type)             15  (INT16)
                     | byte(type)                '@' (INT32)
                     | real(type)                4.0 (REAL32)
                     | string                    "Type Manconst"
                     | TRUE
                     | FALSE

integer          =     digits
                     | #hex.digits

byte             =     'character'

real             =     digits.digits
                     | digits.digitsEexponent

exponent         =     +digits | -digits

digit            =     0 | 1 | 2 | 3 | 4 | 5 | 6 | 7 | 8 | 9

hex.digit        =     digit | A | B | C | D | E | F

string           =     sequence of ASCII characters enclosed in double
                       quotes: "
```

C.6 Declaration

```
declaration      =     type {1 , name }:         INT16 start, end:
```

C.7 Protocol

```
definition       =    PROTOCOL name IS simple.protocol:
                    | PROTOCOL name IS sequential.protocol:
                    | PROTOCOL name
                        CASE
                          { tagged.protocol }
                      :
                                          PROTOCOL To.Other IS INT:
                                          PROTOCOL x.est IS REAL32; REAL32:
                                          PROTOCOL Pixels
                                            CASE
                                              Coords; INT16; INT16; INT16
                                              Mandel; INT16; INT16; INT16
                                              Terminate
                                          :
protocol <4>     =    name
                    | simple.protocol

simple.protocol  =    type <4>                  INT, REAL32
                    | primitive.type::[]type    INT16::[]INT16

input            =    channel ? input.item

input.item       =    variable
                    | variable :: variable    No.P::[Col FROM 0 FOR No.P]

output           =    channel ! output.item

output.item      =    expression
                    | expression :: expression
                                        No.P::[Col FROM 0 FOR No.P]

sequential.
protocol         =    {1 ; simple.protocol }      REAL32; REAL32

input            =    channel ? {1 ; input.item}  Input  ? x; est

output           =    channel ! {1 ; output.item} Output ! x; est

tagged.protocol  =    tag                         Terminate
                    | tag ; sequential.protocol   Coords ; INT16; INT16;
                                                           INT16
tag              =    name

output           =    channel ! tag          ToMandels ! Terminate
                    | channel ! tag ; {1 ; output.item }

                                     ToMandels ! Coords; start; end; row

case.input       =    channel ? CASE  FromMandels ? CASE
                        { variant }     Pixel; start; end; row
                                          ToGraphics ! start; end; row
                                        halt
                                          running := FALSE
```

```
variant          =    tagged.list
                        process
                   |  specification <12>
                      variant
tagged.list      =    tag
                   |  tag ; {1 ; input.item}
process          =    case.input
input            =    channel ? CASE tagged.list
                                          Input ? CASE x.est; x; est
alternative      =    channel ? CASE
                        { variant }
                   |  boolean & channel ? CASE
                        { variant }
```

C.8 Timer access

```
input            =    timer.input
                   |  delayed.input

timer.input      =    timer ? variable            clock ? Start.tick

delayed.input    =    timer ? AFTER expression
```

C.9 Element

```
element          =    element [ subscript ]       Col[12]
                   |  [ element FROM subscript FOR subscript ]
                                                  [Col From 0 FOR No.P]
                   |  name                        est

subscript        =    expression

variable         =    element

channel          =    element

timer            =    element
```

C.10 Expression

```
operand          =    element
                   |  literal                        45
                   |  table                          [x,y,z]
                   |  (expression)                   (x * y)
```

```
expression      =   monadic.operator operand  <16>      -x
                  | operand dyadic.operator operand     x + y
                  | conversion                          INT ROUND n
                  | operand
                  | MOSTPOS type <4>
                  | MOSTNEG type
table           =   table [ subscript]
                  | [{1 , expression}]                  [x, x+2]
                  | [table FROM subscript for count]

conversion      =   primitive.type operand <4>          REAL64 y
                  | primitive.type ROUND operand        INT ROUND (x + y)
                  | primitive.type TRUNC operand        INT32 TRUNC (x * y)
```

C.11 Abbreviation

```
abbreviation    =   specifier name IS element:          INT x IS y:
                  | name IS element:                    Two IS 2:
                  | VAL specifier name IS expression:   VAL R IS 5:
                  | VAL name IS expression:             VAL total IS x + y:

specifier       =   primitive.type <4>                  INT, INT16, REAL32
                  | [] specifier                        [][]REAL32
                  | [ expression] specifier             [x + y] INT16
```

C.12 Scope

```
process         =   specification                       INT x:
                    process <1>                         SEQ
                                                          x := 5
choice          =   specification                           ... etc
                    choice <2>

option          =   specification
                    option <2>

alternative     =   specification
                    alternative <2>

variant         =   specification
                    variant <7>

valof           =   specification
                    valof <14>

specification   =   declaration    <6>
                  | abbreviation   <11>
                  | definition     <7, 13, 14, 15>
```

C.13 Procedure

```
definition        =     PROC name ({0 , formal})
                          procedure.body
                        :

formal            =     specifier {1 , name }  <11>
                      | VAL specifier {1 , name }

procedure.body    =     process      <1, 7, 12, 15>

instance          =     name ({0 , actual})
```

```
Application( To.App, From.App)
```

```
actual            =     element      <9>
                      | expression   <10>
```

C.14 Function

```
value.process     =     valof

valof             =     VALOF
                          process <1, 7, 12, 15>
                          RESULT expression.list
                      | specification <12>
                        valof

operand           =     (value.process
                         )

expression.list   =     (value.process
                        )
```

```
VALOF
  SEQ
    Max := x[0]
    SEQ n = 1 FOR N

      IF
        x[n] > Max
          Max := x[n]
        TRUE
          SKIP
  RESULT Max
```

```
definition        =     {1 , primitive.type} FUNCTION name ({0 , formal})
                          function.body
                        :
```

```
REAL32 FUNCTION Max (VAL[] REAL32 x, VAL INT N)
```

```
function.body     =     value.process

operand           =     name ({0 , expression})

expression.list   =     name ({0 , expression})

definition        =     {1 , primitive.type} FUNCTION name ({0 , formal})
                        IS expression.list:
```

C.15 Configuration

```
placedpar      =  PLACED PAR                  PLACED PAR m = 1 FOR M
                    placedpar                   PROCESSOR m T2
                | PLACED PAR replicator <3> PLACE Pipe[m]   AT linkin:
                    placedper                   PLACE Pipe[m+1] AT linkout:
                | PROCESSOR expression  <1> It (Pipe[m], Pipe[m+1])
                    process

parallel         =    placedpar

parallel         =    PRI PAR
                        process
                    | PRI PAR replicator
                        process

alternation      =    PRI ALT
                        alternative   <2, 7, 12>
                    | PRI ALT replicator <3>
                        alternative

process          =    allocation
                      process

allocation       =    PLACE name AT expression:

definition       =    specifier name RETYPES element: <9>
                    | VAL specifier name RETYPES expression:

                        VAL registers IS [AX,0,col,row,0,0,0,0,0,0]:
                        VAL [] BYTE regs RETYPES registers:

primitive.type   =    PORT OF type <4>

port             =    element

input            =    port ? variable

output           =    port ! expression

protocol         =    ANY
```

C.16 Operators

```
monadic.operator = ~ | << | >>        (BITNOT, left and right shift,
                     | -  | NOT        negative, boolean NOT)

                   AFTER               (later than)

                   SIZE                (array size)
```

```
dyadic.operator  =  + | - | * | / | \            (arithmetic, \ is remainder REM)
                    /\ | \/ | ><                  (BITAND, BITOR, exclusive or)
                    = | < | > | <= | >= | <>      (relational)
                    AND | OR                      (boolean)
                    MINUS | PLUS | TIMES          (modulo)
```

Index to syntax

This second section is an alphabetic index to the sections of the main body of the appendix. For example, `abbreviation 11` indicates that `abbreviation` is found in Section C.11 above.

simple.protocol	7
specification	12
specifier	11
string	5
subscript	9
table	10
tag	7
tagged.list	7
tagged.protocol	7
timer	9
timer.input	8
type	4
valof	12, 14
value.process	14
variable	9
variable.list	1
variant	7, 12

occam2 reserved words

The final part is a list of occam reserved words, again with a reference to the appropriate section of the appendix.

AFTER	later than operator	8
ALT	alternation	2, 3
AND	boolean and operator	16
ANY	anarchic protocol	15
AT	at location	15
BITAND /\	bitwise and operator	16
BITNOT ~	bitwise not operator	16
BITOR \/	bitwise or operator	16
BOOL	boolean type	4
BYTE	byte type	4
CASE	selection, variant protocol, case input	2, 7
CHAN OF	channel type	4
ELSE	default selection	2

FALSE	boolean constant	5
FOR	count	3, 8
FROM	base	8, 9
FUNCTION	function definition	14
IF	conditional	2, 3
IS	specification introduction	7, 11
INT	integer type	4
INT16	16-bit integer type	4
INT32	32-bit integer type	4
INT64	64-bit integer type	4
MINUS	modulo subtraction/ negation operator	16
MOSTNEG	most negative	9
MOSTPOS	most positive	9
NOT	boolean not operator	16
OR	boolean or operator	16
PAR	parallel	2, 3, 15
PLACE	allocation	15
PLACED	placed processes	15
PLUS	modulo addition operator	16
PORT OF	port type	15
PRI	prioritised construction	15
PROC	procedure	13
PROCESSOR	processor allocation	15
PROTOCOL	protocol definition	7
REAL32	32bit real type	4
REAL64	64bit real type	4
REM \	remainder operator	16
RESULT	value process result	14
RETYPES	retyping conversion	15
ROUND	rounding operator	9
SEQ	sequence	2, 3
SIZE	array size operator	16
SKIP	skip process	1, 2
STOP	stop process	1
TIMER	timer type	4

Appendix D

Transputer Development System Aide-memoire

This *aide-memoire* covers almost all the facilities offered by the TDS; some less common ones are omitted.

1. To start:

- ❑ tds2

or

- ❑ tds2 -t fred.top

if you want to create a new .top file.

2. Utilities and conventions

- ❑ Folding Editor (section 3)
- ❑ Loading utilities (section 4)
- ❑ occam program development (compile, run, etc.) (section 5)
- ❑ Transputer development (configure, load network etc.) (section 6)
- ❑ File handling (section 7)

Note: in the following,

❑ Fn refers to function key n

❑ SFn refers to <SHIFT> function key n

❑ ^Fn refers to <CONTROL> function key n

❑ @ refers to ALT key

❑ n refers to digits located above QWERTY

❑ kp refers to key pad

❑ Help key is F1

❑ <TAB> is the tab key

❑ < ←> is the rub out left key, above the <RETURN> key

ALWAYS Ensure the "Numeric Lock" is off, otherwise the keypad keys will not function.

3. Folding Editor (Automatically loaded when you do a tds2)

... – fold line

...F – filed fold

{{{ – top crease

}}} – bottom crease

3.1 moving the cursor

❑ arrow keys

❑ start/end of line – F7/F8

❑ start/end of word – SF7/SF8

❑ page up/down – @F9/@F10

❑ top/bottom of fold – SF9/F10

3.2 deleting/undeleting

Deleting:

❑ a character left/right – <DELETE>/kp.

❑ word left/right – ^F7/^F8

❑ a line – @F7

❑ to EOL – ^kp7

❑ a chunk –
(1) place the chunk in a fold (see section 3.3, below)
(2) delete fold line – @F7

restoring/undeleting a line – @F8 (must be done immediately after a delete)

3.3 Folds (uses "keypad" keys for this section only)

❑ creating a fold -
(1) 0, move to end, 0
(2) type a fold name (if required)

❑ removing a fold -
(1) place cursor on fold line
(2) ^9

❑ entering/opening – 7/1

❑ exiting/closing – 9/3

Entering clears screen and displays contents of fold.

Opening displays contents without clearing screen.

3.4 Indenting/outdenting chunks

(when you have added new occam lines that have disrupted indentation)

(1) place chunk in a fold
(2) insert/delete spaces before ...
(3) remove fold

3.5 Search/replace

(you must load compiler utilities (SF5) to use these – see section 4.1 below)

❑ search – @8 (without replacing)
first time asks for search string
thereafter automatically searches for it
to change one search string for another @F1 (set up edit parameters – see section 4.2 below)

❑ replace – @9
(1) first search – @8
(2) then replace, if you wish (use @8 to move on)

3.6 Copying

❑ a line (to line above) – F4

❑ a line (elsewhere)
(1) copy – F4
(2) press move line – F3
(3) reposition cursor at desired location
(4) F3

❑ multiple copies – repeat all this

❑ a chunk

either
(1) enclose in a fold
(2) move fold as above (a line elsewhere)
(3) remove fold

or
(1) copy pick line repeatedly – @F4
(2) move to new position
(3) put – SF3

This puts picked lines in a buffer fold.

3.7 Filed folds

❑ makes a (disk) file of your chosen fold

❑ file fold – SF2

❑ unfile fold – SF2 (a toggle)

3.8 Quitting the editor/TDS

❑ go to a .TOP level

❑ kp^1

3.9 Leaving edit temporarily (suspend TDS)

(1) kp^3
(2) Do whatever in MS-DOS
(3) EXIT to return to TDS

4. Loading utilities and changing parameters

In addition to the editor, you can load one of three utilities (but only one at a time). These are: file handling; compiler/configurer; and debugger.

4.1 Loading utilities

❑ Autoload

Loads all of them (compiler/configurer, file handler, debugger) -SF5

This leaves you in compiler/configurer.

❑ Change to another utility

@F5 - Toggles between compiler and filer

4.2 Changing utility parameters

Some utility functions (e.g. compile, search) have associated parameters. On first use, the default parameters pop up, for you to change if you wish; if not, just exit fold.

To select a parameter where the options are given, press <TAB> repeatedly.

To quit (without changing) – ^A

Thereafter, they do not pop up again. If you wish to change a parameter, you will find the parameters in the toolkit fold – @F1.

5. Compiling and running on host TDS only

This presumes that there is no network of transputers attached. The host is IBM + B004 only. If there is a network, see section 6.

5.1 A program for the host must be:

```
... EXE somename
```

i.e. executable fold for running on host TDS alone.

❑ Creating an ... EXE fold

First get the compile utilities (@F5)
(1) enter `FOLDNAME.TOP`
(2) make a new fold called "name" (`... name`)
(3) enter it and type in your program
(4) exit fold and file it (`... F name`)
(5) make it an EXE fold
- @7
- replace `PROGRAM` with `EXE`, by using <TAB>
- exit fold.

❑ Removing an EXE fold

Remove fold in usual way (^kp9)

5.2 Syntax checking(before compiling)

(1) place cursor on `... EXE` fold
(2) @1
(3) exit fold (having changed any parameters)

5.3 Compiling

(1) place cursor on `... EXE` fold
(2) @2

5.4 Linking

follows automatically on successful compilation

5.5 Running

(1) place cursor on `... EXE` fold
(2) get code – F5
(3) execute (RUN `EXE`) – F6

5.6 Compilation Units (SC,EXE,PROGRAM)

These are either a

(i) complete occam program (`EXE`, `PROGRAM`), *or*

(ii) separately compiled unit (`SC`) , *or*

(iii) a library (`LIB`)

`SC`s allow parts of a program to be compiled individually, thereby avoiding recompilation, if changes are made elsewhere. The rules are:

– `SC`s consist of one or more procedures

– no global variables etc. allowed

– everything must be passed through parameter list (except `PROTOCOL`s)

– they may be nested.

RECOMPILE UNIT (@5) recompiles an already filed compilation fold (`SC`, `EXE` or `PROGRAM`), using appropriate compiler (for T2, T4 etc.)

– default does not search for nested SCs

❑ **Creating a compilation fold (SC, EXE, PROGRAM)**

(1) put cursor on an already filed fold
(2) @7 (careful not @F7)
(3) change to `SC`, `EXE`, `PROGRAM` as required (<TAB>)
(4) leave fold

❑ **Removing an EXE, SC, PROGRAM fold**

Simply remove fold (^kp9)

5.7 Make comment

- use to temporarily remove code from program (e.g. whilst debugging)

(1) position cursor (having created a fold around chunk if required)
(2) @0

– to remove, use remove fold.

6. Configuring, loading and running programs for a network

To run programs with a network, they first have to be configured and then loaded on to the network. You can run a network either in conjunction with the TDS on the host, or without as a "stand-alone" program.

Configuring assigns processes to processors in a network of transputers; and assigns channels to links in the network.

With TDS ("stand-alone" is covered below):

6.1 A program must be:

`... EXE` – which runs on the host.

`... PROGRAM`– which runs on the network.

(see section 5.6 on how to make fold sets)

To run a compiled and configured (see section 6.2) program:

(1) load `...` `PROGRAM` onto the network (see section 6.3)
(2) get `... EXE`
(3) run `... EXE`

or (2), (1), then (3); BUT NOT (2), (3), (1)!

6.2 Configuring

Creates information for controlling the distribution of compiled occam programs onto a network of transputers. This information is used when loading the programs onto the network.

(1) place cursor on `... PROGRAM` fold
(2) @ 2 (This also first compiles, if needed)

❑ NOTE: Configuring is automatically followed by extracting (see section 6.5). The first time you use it you may have to select its parameters:

"output.fold" – BOOTABLE

"boot.from.link" – TRUE

6.3 Loading Network

❑ Sends compiled code to the network of transputers from the host, via a link (default 2):

(1) place cursor on `... PROGRAM` fold
(2) @ 4

❑ NOTE: The first time you use it you may have to select the parameters offered.

6.4 Configuration Information

❑ Produces a fold (`...F CONFIG INFO PROGRAM name` inside the `... PROGRAM` fold) containing:

(i) load map for each transputer

(ii) boot path for each transputer via which links

(iii) link wiring diagram between transputers

(1) place cursor on `... PROGRAM` fold
(2) @6

6.5 Extract

❑ Produces a fold (`...F CODE PROGRAM name`, inside the `... PROGRAM` fold) containing:

(i) routing information

(ii) bootstraps and code to load network

❑ Loading a network is quicker from an extracted fold.

(1) place cursor on `... PROGRAM` fold
(2) @3

NOTE: The first time you extract, select the parameters BOOTABLE and boot.from.link.

6.6 Interrupting a program

❑ <CONTROL><BREAK> (simultaneously)

6.7 Rerunning a program

❑ must first reload network and then get and run as in section 6.1

Stand-alone

Since the program is to run independently of the TDS, it will need modification (not covered in this *Aide-memoire*) to run with a SERVER program. The host transputer can still be used as a processor as part of the network, but the TDS will not be running on it. Development work of a program is still done using the TDS, and when ready, the program can then be run without the TDS.

To run, leave the TDS and in MS-DOS afserver -:b name.b4

6.8 A program must be:

`... PROGRAM` – which runs on the network (i.e. no `...EXE` fold)

6.9 Configuring

as above - section 6.2.

6.10 Extracting

as above - section 6.3.

The `PROGRAM` must be extracted so the extraction code can be written to the file name.b4, run by the afserver. The afserver also loads the network, and boots the transputers in the network.

6.11 Writing name.b4

(1) get file utilities
(2) enter `... PROGRAM` fold
(3) place cursor on `...F CODE PROGRAM` fold
(4) write to MS-DOS - @0

6.12 Leave the TDS and run as above

afserver -:b name.b4

7. File handling

❑ copying of files from within one .TOP to itself or another

❑ file renaming

❑ file protection

❑ copying TDS files between directories

❑ conversion between MS-DOS and TDS files

To use get FILE by selecting NEXT UTIL (@F5)

7.1 Copying of files within one .TOP

(1) create an empty fold with the same name and extension as the one you want to copy from
(2) @2
(3) change the name of the new file, otherwise you may have problems with inadvertent deletions. Type in new name, then @4

(NOTE: only .EXE or .TSR folds can be copied, not .TOP folds)

❑ copies all nested files, too.

7.2 Protection

@5 – sets a file so it cannot be changed or deleted.

@6 – removes it.

7.3 Getting hard copy of programs etc.

(1) move cursor to file fold
(2) @0
(3) give a name
(4) exit fold.

(NOTE: you are asked for a new name every time you use this function)

There are various other file handling facilities which are not frequently used.

IBM/Transputer Keyboard Layout

Function keys usage

F1	F2	F3	F4	F5	F6	F7	F8	F9	F10	
						Delete Word Left	Delete Word Right			HOLD ← CTRL
	File/ Unfile	Put		Auto Load Compiler		Move Word Left	Move Word Right	Top of fold	Bottom of fold	HOLD ← SHIFT
Tool-kit	Code Info	Pick Line	Copy Pick	Next UTIL	Next EXE	Delete Line	Un-delete Line	Page↑	Page↓	HOLD ← ALT
Help	Fold Info	Move Line	Copy Line	Get Code	Run EXE	Start of Line	End of Line	Line↑	Line↓	

Numeric Keys Usage

Load each utility from AUTOLOAD (SF5)

Compiler & Configurer Utilities (ALT+Numeric)

1 Check	4 Load Network	7 Make foldset	0 Make Comment
2 Compile/configure	5 Recompile	8 Search	
3 Extract	6 Compile Info	9 Replace	

Filing Utilities (ALT+Numeric)

1 Attach	4 Rename file	7 Copy in	0 Write Host
2 Copy attach	5 Write Protect	8 Copy Out	
3 Compact libs	6 Write Enable	9 Read Host	

Other keys

<TAB> – seslect parameter
<Delete> – delete left
<CNTRL>A – set abort

7 Enter Fold	8 ↑	9 Exit Fold
4 ←	5	6 →
1 Open Fold	2 ↓	3 Close Fold
0 Create Fold	Delete Right	

<CNTRL>

7 Delete to EOL	8	9 Remove Fold
4 Move Word Left	5	6 Move Word Right
1 Finish TDS	2	3 Suspend TDS

Index